Hysteria, it's not funny on HRT

The Information Needs of Women Having a Hysterectomy

A dissertation submitted for the Master of Science at Loughborough University 1997

Linda Parkinson-Hardman (was Linda Newall)

ISBN 13: 978-1-7394272-0-7

Published by: Crystal Clear Books

Website: www.lindaph.co.uk

FOREWORD (2023)

Twenty five years ago I completed this work and submitted it to gain a masters degree at Loughborough University. It has taken this long to finally publish it in it's extant form. The reasons for this are many, suffice it to say that this is not, necessarily, the end of the story.

As the original work was coming to a close, I was approached by a number of the research participants who were concerned that they would lose access to the example website I created as part of the project. They felt the information had been useful to them and would be useful to others in the coming years.

The result of those conversations was the creation of The Hysterectomy Association which took the original online pages and developed them into an information resources used by over two million women every year at its peak. This early work formed the basis of my first book, The Pocket Guide to Hysterectomy. Following the websites success, I went on to publish three more books for women, the most popular is now in its fifth edition and is titled 101 Handy Hints for a Happy Hysterectomy.

The website morphed from a simple set of online pages coded by hand, into a fully functional content management system with forums hosting hundereds of thousands of threads and conversations, proving the point of the work, that women needed a place to learn about what it means to have a hysterectomy. What surprised me over the years was the number of men using the site to find out more information for their wives, partners, mothers and sisters. Over the course of the site's lifetime I could count on the fingers of one hand the number of times the conversation got out of hand and where I had to intervene in some way.

Whilst this work is inevitably dated, it serves as a useful history of both the way in which patient health information has evolved over the course of the last quarter century, and how the internet and web became the game-changer that has shaped our understanding of both health and medicine.

Many of the issues raised within this study are still with us today and are being exacerbated either deliberately, or as an unintended consequence of the way the technology has moved from being a democratising force to one shaped almost entirely by commercial interests. It is as difficult today to discern good health information from bad, as it was when the web was still in its infancy. The rise of censorship and an exhortation to 'follow the science' regardless that the science has been co-opted and captured entirely by those self-same commercial interests has resulted in a more fractured and challenging information landscape than was envisaged by Tim Berners-Lee when the web was first enabled.

I learnt a lot through The Hysterectomy Association. Not least that the Western style medical model is more broken than I hinted at in the original research. As a result, I closed the association in 2019, although the archive of central pages still remains online for use by anyone who cares to find it at www.hysterectomy-association.org.uk.

There is a significant body of research data gathered from the twenty fives years the association existed. The original survey used in this research was repeated over the course of about ten years with thousands of respondents. Additional research surveys were also developed considering the short, medium and long term effects of hysterectomy, and finally the role abuse might play in the eventual need for surgery. At some point I may analyse and publish the results of these research efforts.

The core information about hysterectomy, the menopause and hormone replacement therapy mostly still stands, although there have been developments in surgical techniques as well as our understanding of the risks and benefits of HRT. It is with this in mind I urge anyone reading this to check out this information against that which has been added to the archive mentioned above, and with their own GP if necessary.

If you would like to contact me to ask a question or to comment on this publication you can do so by email to linda@lindaph.co.uk.

Additional works by Linda Parkinson-Hardman (was Newall)

- The Pocket Guide to Hysterectomy
- 101 Handy Hints for a Happy Hysterectomy
- Losing the Woman Within
- In My Own Words: Women's experience of hysterectomy

FOREWORD (1997)

Hysterectomy is one of the most common surgical procedures for women in Britain today. Statistics indicate that by the age of 75, one in five women will have had their uterus removed. However, many women find that there is a lack of information about the procedure and the implications for their long term health.

In addition to the lack of information about hysterectomy, there is also a dearth of easily understood information on the most frequently prescribed drug for these women, hormone replacement therapy. Many women who undergo a hysterectomy are prescribed this drug particularly if they had their operation before they would naturally have gone through the menopause

There are many good books and leaflets on the procedure of hysterectomy and also on hormone replacement therapy, there is little that combines the two, that is specifically aimed at post-hysterectomised women. In order to consider the types of information that women receive currently and would like to be given, a questionnaire was devised and sent out five groups of women, who came from two GP surgeries, Women's Health organisation and Here's Health magazine and some who contacted me personally. The data was analysed and considered and two information resources for women were produced; a Web site and a Booklet.

The website that accompanies the study can be found at: **http://web.ukonline.co.uk/linda.newall/index.html**.

Although there is little use of the Internet at present, there is evidence that it is growing rapidly and one of the most prolific areas already supported by the Internet is health information. The site will be kept up to date following the conclusion of the study.

The booklet is located at the end of this dissertation. The information contained within it is the same as that found on the web site, but with less detail. The booklet has been created to show how this type of information could be presented.

Both methods of communication have pro's and con's. The web site provides instant publication world-wide, is free to the user and requires no sponsorship, however the audience it reaches at present is limited. The booklet can reach more women but relies on sponsorship or self publication and there will be some cost to the user.

Acknowledgements

I would like to thank my supervisor Janet Rollinson, for her timely help and guidance with more than my dissertation.

I would also like to thank Dr Livingstone and Dr Corfield for their help.

I would also like recognition for those women that took part and those who contacted me, they provided the raw data for the study.

Please Note:

The original research and publishing of the dissertation was undertaken under a previous surname.

Throughout the work the term Hormone Replacement Therapy is abbreviated to HRT.

Hormone Replacement Therapy is the British title, in the US the term is Estrogen Replacement Therapy or ERT

Oestrogen is the English spelling and Estrogen is the American-English spelling.

Some original appendices have been removed as they are no longer relevant.

The original website was on a personal site that no longer functions. Snapshots of it can be found on the Wayback machine at the Internet Archive.

Many of the resources mentioned in the work are no longer available, have changed or merged with other organisations.

Contents

List Of Figures

List Of Tables

Introduction

The Patient's Charter enshrines the right to receive information about any conditions and medical procedures that are proposed. This should include information on any risks associated with the treatment and any alternatives available. It also requires that healthcare professionals ensure that it is all clearly explained before the treatment takes place.

However, it appears that the information that is available to women about hysterectomy, its' alternatives and the consequences is not given in any great detail. Hysterectomy is one of the most common surgical procedures for women in Britain today. Statistics indicate that by the age of 75, one in five women will have had their womb removed. Doctors and medical staff may not always have the time or the facilities to give enough detail and at the same time many women find it difficult to talk about because of its emotional as well as physical implications.

In addition to the above there is also a lack of easily understood information on the most frequently prescribed drug for these women, Hormone Replacement Therapy. Many women who undergo a hysterectomy are prescribed this type of drug, particularly if they had their operation before they would naturally have gone through the Menopause because healthcare professionals recognise the threat to their long term health without it. However, most women are only aware of the headlines that surround the topic and it is becoming increasingly controversial. It would be foolish not to acknowledge that there are considerations that all women must take into account before they embark on long-term drug therapy, but these should be considered before the operation even takes place and must be understood by the woman undergoing the surgery. Unless the surgery is life saving, and that is rarely the case with hysterectomy, all implications should be considered before treatment. This of course is only possible if there is adequate un-biased information available to women from the outset, preferably from their GP's surgery.

Although there are many good books and leaflets on the procedure of hysterectomy, covering both the physical and mental implications; and there are also many good books and leaflets that look at the issues of Hormone Replacement Therapy for post-menopausal women, there is a dearth of information that combines the two. Women that have a hysterectomy that removes their ovaries will go through the menopause immediately, regardless of their age, women that have a hysterectomy that retains one or both of their ovaries have a 50% chance of going through the menopause within two to five years of their operation (again regardless of their age).

There are also specific health implications for women that have this operation, particularly those that have a hysterectomy in the years before the menopause because their oestrogen and testosterone levels drop, this affects both the heart and the bones. Much of the information about Hormone Replacement Therapy is written from the perspective of a woman that has gone through the menopause naturally and women that have had a hysterectomy who read it may imply that they will have the same responses in physical terms that any other woman undergoing menopause has, this is not usually the case.

The issues are very different. For instance women who have the surgical removal of some or all of their reproductive organs may be on this drug for significantly longer than other women. They also take it to manage more serious health concerns, such as heart disease and osteoporosis. Their counterparts going through the menopause naturally take the drug mainly for the relief of menopausal symptoms. In addition to oestrogen they also take progesterone.

Background Information

I underwent a hysterectomy at the age of 32. I became concerned because, through my own research, I find that the operation I had may have been unnecessary. The information I was given was scanty and I had to make many enquiries myself. As a result of this personal experience I believe that other women would like more information that is easy to read and that discusses the issues that concern them. This of course does not apply to all women, as there are patients that will always rely on the advice of the professionals and who have little interest in managing their own health.

Aims

The aims of the project are:

1. to document the types of information currently available to women having a hysterectomy,
2. to determine the type of information that women require to help them make an informed choice about having a hysterectomy,

3. to produce an information resource that provides information on all issues of interest to women having a hysterectomy.

Objectives

The aims of this study will be supported by the following actions:

- by analysing the information currently supplied to women by healthcare professionals
- by analysing information given by GP's concerning the queries that women raise regarding their treatment
- by analysing information given by women about the questions they have regarding their treatment
- by gathering the most up to date information in the following key areas:
    - Hysterectomy
    - Menopause
    - Hormone Replacement Therapy
- by the production of a booklet in line with the patients requirements.
- by the production of a WWW page with the opportunity for feedback about the information given on it. The WWW page will be maintained after the study has finished.

Deliverables

- A quality WWW resource for women looking for information on hysterectomy and hormone replacement.
- An information booklet that may be used by GP's to give information to their patients.
- A dissertation detailing the processes that have taken place to arrive at the other deliverables.

Methodology

The study will be conducted over a six month period, February - September 1997. There will be no control groups used because of the short time frame and due to the fact that the study is attempting only to document current practice and identify possible areas for change rather than to actually initiate the change itself.

The postal questionnaire is the survey technique being used to gather quantitative data. This technique allows the maintenance of a consistent format, will help to ensure a reduction in bias and allows the collection of large amounts of data in the short time frame. All data will be anonomised in the final report. As the respondents are likely to be dispersed geographically, the data will be gathered at no cost to them by using stamped addressed envelopes for the questionnaires return.

The structure of work will be as follows:-

1. Gather data showing the types of information either given to women or available for them about their hysterectomy.
2. Send questionnaires for GP's taking part to complete.
3. Send questionnaires to the women taking part, either through their GP or directly.
4. Analyse the data with SPSS and Excel.
5. Produce the Information Resources, Internet and Booklet.

1. The Issues Of Hysterectomy

1.1 Hysterectomy

Up to 60,000 hysterectomy operations are carried out on women in the UK every year, this figure represents one in five of all women[1]. It can, and does help to ease many gynaecological complaints, including heavy and/or painful periods, endometriosis, prolapse etc. It is rarely performed for reasons of saving life, but it can be a permanent cure for some gynaecological cancers.

The majority of hysterectomies are performed when a woman is aged between 40-50[2], however many do occur before and after this age group. Women who have a hysterectomy that removes their ovaries, as well as other organs, will go through the menopause immediately (if they haven't already) following the operation regardless of their age. Women who have a hysterectomy that leaves one or both of their ovaries intact have a 50% chance of going through the menopause within two to five years of their operation[3], this is again regardless of their age.

1.1.1 What Is A Hysterectomy?

Hysterectomy is defined as the "surgical removal of the uterus" (womb)[4]. It is one of the most common of all surgical procedures and can also involve the removal of the fallopian tubes, ovaries and cervix to cure or alleviate a number of gynaecological complaints. Following this operation women will no longer have periods, will not be fertile and will not be able to have any more children.

There are two main operations for hysterectomy. The most common way is to remove the uterus through a cut in the lower abdomen, the second less common, way is to remove the uterus only through a cut in the top of the vagina, the top of vagina is then stitched. Each operation lasts between one to two hours and is performed, in hospital, under a general anaesthetic.

The type of hysterectomy a woman will have will depend upon the condition it is being used to treat.

- A "subtotal hysterectomy" removes the uterus leaving the cervix in place. Women that have this operation continue to have smear tests.
- A "total hysterectomy" removes the complete uterus including the cervix, this is the operation most commonly performed.
- A "total hysterectomy with bilateral or unilateral salpingo-oopherectomy" removes the uterus, cervix, fallopian tubes and both or one of the ovaries.
- A "wertheims hysterectomy" removes the uterus, cervix, part of the vagina, fallopian tubes, peritoneum (this is the broad band of ligament below the uterus), the lymph glands and fatty tissue of the pelvis and possibly one or both ovaries.

1.1.2 Why Do Women Need A Hysterectomy?

Hysterectomy sometimes becomes necessary for the following medical reasons:

- Heavy vaginal bleeding or bleeding that is irregular or very painful
- Fibroids which cause pain, bleeding or are very large. A fibroid is a non-cancerous growth of muscle and fibrous tissue.
- Cancer of the uterus, ovaries, fallopian tube/s or cervix
- Edometriosis caused by tissues that normally form inside the uterus forming outside the uterus in the abdominal cavity.
- Prolapse of the uterus, where the uterus falls into the vagina.
- Pelvic inflammatory disease or adhesions which has pain that is not controlled by other means.

A hysterectomy may be recommended if none of the initial treatments for these conditions has been successful. Some of the conditions, such as Endometriosis and Pelvic Inflammatory Disease, may clear up on their own or after a D&C operation (Dilation and Curettage where the lining of the uterus is scraped away and if necessary examined).

Heavy Vaginal Bleeding

Heavy vaginal bleeding usually refers to heavy periods (Menorrhagia), although it can also mean bleeding between periods and/or periods lasting longer than a week. The amount of blood lost will depend upon hormone levels throughout a woman's cycle. Bleeding differs between women and the perception of what is a heavy bleed is often very difficult to diagnose, what is heavy for one woman, may be fairly light for another.

A heavy period is usually one that lasts longer than seven days or if large clots of blood are passed or if flooding occurs. It can be a symptom of other conditions, such as endometriosis, fibroids or pelvic inflammatory disease and it is possible that having a coil fitted for contraceptive purposes can make periods heavier and/or more painful. They can also be caused by high levels of the female sex hormones or by an imbalance in the prostaglandin's, which are naturally occurring substance in the body[5] .

Initial treatment with hormones or the contraceptive pill and iron tablets may be tried. If this is unsuccessful then a "trans-cervical re-section" of the lining of the uterus may be performed which removes the lining of the womb.

Fibroids

A fibroid is a benign tumour of the uterus and they will often appear either within the muscular wall of the uterus or on the outside of the wall. The rate at which they grow depends on individual women.

It is estimated that between 25 - 35% of all women will have fibroids in varying sizes[6]. It is possible to treat small fibroids by passing an instrument through the cervix into the uterus and cutting them away or by D&C (Dilation and curettage), it is also sometimes possible to treat individual fibroids with an operation called a Myomectomy which involves cutting through the abdomen into the uterus.

Gynaecological Cancers

There are four main cancer's of the female reproductive organs; cancer of the uterus, cancer of the fallopian tubes, cervical cancer and ovarian cancer.

Cancer of the uterus starts in the lining of the endometrium and may then spread to the fallopian tubes, ovaries and the lymphatic system. The symptoms may include bleeding between periods or spotting if you have already gone through the menopause. There may also be a pink to brown discharge and intermittent period-like pains. It is the fifth most common cancer amongst women[7], and it occurs mainly in women between the ages of 50-60 who have not had children. Unfortunately there are no early detection tests for this type of cancer, however as the cancer grows very slowly, it is essential that any symptoms are reported as early as possible.

Cancer of the fallopian tubes is very rare. It accounts for around 0.1 to 0.5% of all gynaecological cancers. Patients may have a watery vaginal discharge, pelvic pain, vaginal bleeding and a small lump. The cancer grows very slowly and as bleeding occurs quite early on it is usually easy to detect and remove before it spreads to the lymph nodes and ovaries.

Cervical cancer most often develops in women who have changes in the skin on the outside of the cervix, this is why it is important to ensure that regular smear tests are carried out. The main symptoms are a watery, bloody discharge which may smell and bleeding between periods or after the menopause or after sex. Although it is one of the most common cancers in women, affecting 1 woman in 80 with 2000 women dying every year, it is one of the easiest to diagnose, treat and cure if it detected early enough.

Ovarian cancer causes the deaths of up to 4,000 women every year, although it is rare in women under the age of 40. It is caused when abnormal tissue develops in the ovary and is sometimes related to ovarian cysts. It is very difficult to detect in it's early stages because the ovaries are buried in the abdominal cavity. Any swelling is often not noticed until the disease is very far advanced, it is at this stage that there may be other symptoms including lower abdominal pain weight loss and general ill-health.

Endometriosis

Endometriosis is caused when the cells of the endometrium (lining of the uterus) are found in other parts of the body. In the same way that the lining of the uterus swells and sheds each month as a bleed, these growths also swell and bleed, but as they are embedded in tissue, the blood cannot escape and so it forms blood blisters that will in turn irritate and scar the surrounding tissue which will then form a fibrous cyst around the blister.

It is believed to be caused by a "retrograde menstruation"[8], where fragments of the lining are shed backwards rather than through the vagina. Women may suffer no symptoms at all or they may be in great pain when they have a period or during sex and periods may be very heavy. Initial treatment will be with hormone drugs that either reduce or stop the periods altogether and which allow the blisters to heal, however if the ovaries are affected then removal may be necessary.

Prolapse

Prolapse of the uterus or vagina occurs when the muscles and ligaments holding these organs in place become weak. Stretching and slackening is a natural result of childbirth and also takes place as the woman gets older. When the muscles and ligaments no longer work the uterus and vagina will sag down and a bulge of the bladder or rectum will occur in the front or back wall of the vagina. It can also occur due to a thinning of the muscles at the time of the menopause which, in turn, is caused by a drop in the female sex hormones.

Symptoms may include a lump or bulge in the side of vagina, discomfort in the vagina, backache and possible problems with the bladder or rectum. Self help measures include dieting, eating plenty of high fibre foods to prevent constipation and straining, and pelvic floor exercises. A repair operation will also be necessary when organs other than just the uterus are involved[9].

Pelvic Inflammatory Disease

Pelvic inflammatory disease (P.I.D.) or salpingitis occurs when microbes get into the uterus and spread to the fallopian tubes, ovaries and surrounding tissues. It is often, but not always, introduced during sex (through sexually transmitted diseases such as gonorrhoea) and may occur after surgery in the abdomen. Symptoms may include pain and/or tenderness in the lower abdomen, low grade fever, backache, discharge and problems with periods may occur. Antibiotics can be prescribed initially and painkillers can be taken to relieve the pain. If the symptoms continue it may be necessary to have a laparoscopy (a small incision is made in the abdomen and a camera is inserted into the uterus) in hospital to check on the diagnosis.

1.1.3 How Hysterectomy Affects Women

How a woman feels after having had a hysterectomy will depend a great deal on her personal circumstances and why the operation became necessary in the first place.

Physically there are a number of issues that are common to all women having a hysterectomy. She will of course no longer menstruate and will not be able to have children any more. If her ovaries were removed then she will go through the menopause, regardless of her age because the menopause is not related to age it is related to the production of the female sex hormone, oestrogen. If a woman has not had her ovaries removed and she has not yet gone through the menopause, there will be up to a 50% chance that she will also go through the menopause within two to five years of having the operation[10]. It can take up to two years to recover fully from the surgery.

Sexually, she may resume intercourse after about six weeks, however many women may find that it is different in some ways depending again on why the operation was necessary and the type of operation undertaken. Although some women report that their sex life improves following a hysterectomy, as they are not experiencing great pain any longer, others report that they have different types or intensity of orgasm. The latter is probably due to the fact that the it isn't just the clitoris that is involved in creating an orgasm, but the womb and cervix also as they are contractual muscles. Therefore, orgasm may be less intense when they have been removed[11].

It is also possible that a deficiency of the hormone, oestrogen, will affect a woman's sexuality. It is well documented that one of the symptoms of the menopause is dryness of the vagina and this is alleviated by taking oestrogen. We are now aware that the hormone, testosterone, also plays a part in female sexuality. With the removal of both of these hormones then, it could explain a lack of sexual interest, frequency and orgasm[12].

Emotionally, women may feel a sense of depression following surgery due in some part to the major surgery, although some women report a feeling of loss as they are aware that they can no longer have children or that they feel they are no longer "womanly". It has also been suggested that some of these feelings may be due to a lack of oestrogen and testosterone and are symptoms of the menopause.

1.2 The Menopause

If a woman has had her ovaries removed during the surgery then she will have an immediate menopause, regardless of her age. If she had a hysterectomy that retained the ovaries there is a 50% chance of those ovaries failing within two - five years of the hysterectomy[13], this may be due to the blood supply to the uterus being cut off[14]. Radiation treatment following hysterectomy for cancer may also cause the ovaries to fail prematurely[15].

Following a natural menopause, the ovaries continue to play a part in a woman's health as they continue to produce a small amount of oestrogen and a more significant amount of testosterone for up to 12 years. Therefore there are indications that women having a hysterectomy should be offered the supplementation of testosterone as well as oestrogen[16].

The term menopause is defined as the final bleed a woman will have[17]. It is an entirely natural event and every woman will experience it, if she lives long enough. The word "menopause" is often used to define the period of time that leads up to a woman's' final period, although this is strictly a period of time called the "peri-menopause". The final menstrual period takes place, usually between the ages of 45 and 55, although it can be earlier or later and the peri-menopause can begin as early as ten years before the final bleed. The peri-menopause is caused when the two ovarian hormones, oestrogen and progesterone are no longer stimulating the endometrium to prepare for eggs.

The menopause then, has three phases to it:

- peri-menopause
- menopause
- post-menopause

The whole of this period can be referred to as "the climacteric" from the Greek "klimakterikos" which means rung of a ladder[18].

1.2.1 Menopausal Symptoms

Strictly speaking, the symptoms of the menopause are those that identify the time leading up to the final bleed and this is usually called the peri-menopause. Symptoms can be both physical and psychological in nature.

Some of the symptoms are described as "acute" and these are those that will occur immediately there is a reduction in the production of oestrogen. These include hot flushes, night sweats, dry vagina, dry hair and skin, insomnia, bladder problems and moodiness. The remainder are described as "chronic" and take place over a longer period of time. These include irregular periods, breast changes and other psychological symptoms. All women that have a hysterectomy that removes their ovaries will begin to experience acute symptoms, even as early as 24 hours following surgery. Women whose operation has left their ovaries intact have a 50% chance of experiencing acute symptoms within five years of their surgery. A simple blood test can be performed to measure the level of oestrogen in the blood.

Physical symptoms may include:

Irregular periods: they may vary in timing, they may be lighter or heavier and they may be a combination of these. Whatever the age of the woman heavy bleeding may also be a sign of something more serious and should be referred to a Doctor.

Hot and cold flushes: sweating during the day and at night and palpitations are all known as Vasomotor symptoms. Exact causes of the vasomotor symptoms are unknown but it is thought probable that the hypothalamus, which regulates body temperature, is affected by the decrease in oestrogen production and this in turn dilates the blood vessels when it affects the sympathetic nervous system[19]. It is thought that up to 80% of women will experience vasomotor symptoms[20].

Insomnia and headaches are secondary vasomotor symptoms which can also occur as a result of night sweats which result in loss of sleep.

Changes in the vagina include a shortening in length, weakening of the skin, diminishing blood supply, changes in the acidity levels and dryness due to the reduction in secretions from the mucous glands. All of these can lead to pain on sex and increase the risk of bleeding and infection.

The bladder and urethra are also affected as the linings become thin and weak and stress incontinence can occur as they atrophy. This increases the risk of infection and bleeding.

Breast changes are as a direct result of the reduction in production of oestrogen. The breasts may become smaller and less elastic and the skin will become thinner and dryer.

The skin and hair become dryer and the elasticity of the skin reduces which increases the appearance of wrinkles. The changes in the skin are due to damaging effects on the connective tissue (collagen) when oestrogen production reduces.

Psychological Symptoms are similar to those experienced with pre-menstrual Syndrome and may include mood swings, irritability, anxiety, poor concentration, poor memory, loss of energy and depression. It cannot be confirmed at present whether these symptoms are caused by oestrogen deprivation or whether they are as a result of other physical symptoms, such as lack of sleep. However, as some sleep disorders are helped by hormone replacement therapy it would appear that there is a link with oestrogen deficiency.

1.3 Osteoporosis

Osteoporosis is defined as "the wasting away of bone"[21], and the term literally means "porous bones". It is often called the silent epidemic as many people can be unaware of its onset and the first indication of the disease can be falling and breaking a bone. It has been considered a natural part of ageing, although with treatment it is largely preventable. Dr Frederick S Kaplan, a professor of orthopaedic surgery at the University of Pennsylvania has described osteoporosis in the following way:

> *"if hypertension is a silent killer, osteoporosis is a silent thief. It insidiously robs the skeleton of its banked resources, often for decades, until the bone is weak enough to sustain a spontaneous fracture"*[22] .

Osteoporosis is most common in the elderly and in post-menopausal women. It is caused by the loss of calcium from the bones. Bones continue to grow and develop throughout childhood and adolescence and the bones are at their most dense around the age of 30[23], after this the bone mass gradually diminishes. The Royal College of Physicians in the United Kingdom has indicated that the incidence of hip fractures has risen by 254% between 1954 and 1983 and has been rising ever since[24]. Dr Sandra Cabot states that the disease currently affects one in every three women in western society[25]. This could be due to the change to a less healthy diet with less calcium or it could be linked to the increase in hysterectomies performed.

1.3.1 Risk Factors

Andrew Hampson has identified oestrogen deficiency in women as one of the most important factors in the development of osteoporosis for women[26], and John Studd has stated that women undergoing hysterectomy before they would normally go through the menopause are "*more likely to develop osteoporosis*" than those in the same age group[27]. Oestrogen deficiency occurs after the onset of the menopause[28]. However, although oestrogen deficiency is a major factor there are others to take into account these include:

- Race; white or Asian people are slightly more at risk.
- Build; fine boned people will have a higher risk.
- Smoking.
- Being underweight.
- Diet consistently low in calcium and high in phosphates.
- Excessive alcohol and caffeine intake.
- Family history of osteoporosis.
- Lack of exercise.
- Use of cortisone-like drugs.
- Vitamin deficiency.
- Being female; it is estimated to be six to eight times more common in women than in men as women have a lower bone mass to start with.[29,30] .

1.3.2 Types Of Osteoporosis

There are two types of osteoporosis. Type one is caused by a lack of sex hormones and results in loss of the inner layer of bone called the trabecular bone. Type two is caused mainly by a lack of calcium and/or vitamin D in the diet, this causes a loss of the outer layer of the bone called the cortical bone[31].

A woman who goes through the menopause early, perhaps due to having had a hysterectomy will therefore, be more at risk of type one osteoporosis as she will have longer without oestrogen. Women that have consistently light periods and/or have a time without menstruating at all will also be more at risk from this type of osteoporosis.

Cells called osteoblasts work on the creation of new bone and cells called osteoclasts work to reabsorb calcium into the blood. It is this reabsorbtion or calcium into the blood stream that causes osteoporosis. There are three hormones that control the calcium levels in the blood, they are the parathyroid hormone, 1,25 dihydroxy-vitamin D and calcitonin. They also control the uptake of calcium by the bones. The rate of absorption varies through out life and is decreased by the risk factors outlined above and increased at times of hormone increase such as during pregnancy.

1.3.3 Prevention

It has been recommended that all women have a bone mineral density (BMD) test before they undergo a hysterectomy, this will determine how strong the bones are to start with and will provide a point of reference for later on. Regular blood tests to determine continuing levels of oestrogen are also recommended, particularly if there has been a hysterectomy leaving ovaries intact.

The most common way to prevent osteoporosis due to poor oestrogen levels is to boost the levels with HRT. This puts oestrogen back into the body, that would normally have been produced by the ovaries. It has been shown to retard, stop and even reverse bone loss after the menopause[32]. It is recommended that HRT is taken for a period of not less than ten years, if it is taken after a natural menopause, to give a maximum effect of prevention[33].

Exercise is also recommended as this helps to strengthen bones. However, the type of exercise is very important, it should be regular and it should be weight bearing. Weight bearing exercises include any type of exercise that involves upright movement so that pressure is exerted through the spine, pelvis and legs and includes walking, jogging, aerobics and yoga.

Diet is also particularly important, it should contain high levels of calcium and vitamin D (Vitamin D can also be obtained from being out in the sunshine) and should be low in fat and high in fibre.

1.4 Heart Disease

Around 45% of British women will suffer from heart disease or a stroke and it is the biggest single cause of death in the UK in post-menopausal women[34,35]. Up to the time of the menopause, women appear to have a natural immunity to heart disease unlike their male counterparts. It appears that the incidence of heart disease is around a third of the level of men's'. However, after the age of menopause the incidence gradually increases to come into line with men at around the age of 75. According to John Studd, hysterectomy in pre-menopausal women is associated with a three-fold increased risk of coronary heart disease and this is the case even when the ovaries are left intact[36].

We can also assume that if a woman has a hysterectomy and consequently goes through the menopause early, the age at which she comes into line with male incidence of heart disease will be correspondingly lower.

1.4.1 Risk Factors

Oestrogen affects the blood cholesterol levels and also regulates the circulation of LDL (low-density lipoproteins - "bad" cholesterol) and HDL (high density lipoproteins - "good" cholesterol). After the menopause the blood cholesterol and LDL levels go up and the HDL levels drop, this encourages an increase in the hardening of arteries and is particularly pronounced in women that smoke, are overweight and do not take regular exercise.

In addition to heart disease, insulin resistance also increases following menopause; this in turn can lead to an increased risk of heart disease itself. Insulin resistance can lead to type II diabetes. The link between insulin resistance and heart disease is due to high levels of LDL and low levels of HDL.

Particularly at risk are the following groups:

- Smokers.
- People that are overweight.

- Families with a history of heart disease.
- High levels of cholesterol before the hysterectomy.
- People that do not take regular exercise.

1.4.2 Prevention

Most people dislike the idea of taking any form of medication for a long time, but one of the major benefits of taking HRT is that it is probably the single most effective way of preventing heart disease as it returns the body to it's pre-menopause state. According to Dr Sandra Cabot

> *"the risk of cardiovascular disease can be reduced by 50% by taking oestrogen at or soon after the menopause"*[37].

The Framlingham Heart study looked at 48,000 nurses and found that after 10 years there were half as many deaths from cardiovascular disease amongst those women that took oestrogen only HRT after their menopause as opposed to those that did not take any form of HRT[38,39]. According to Bailey, David Morris has stated that the protective effect of oestrogen only hormone replacement therapy is also found in those women that already have the disease[40].

Fortunately women that have had a menopause do not need to take progesterone as well as oestrogen in their HRT. This is fortunate because there seems to be some indication that progesterone has the effect of reducing the benefits of oestrogen as well as having a possibly detrimental effect on the endometrium[41].

1.5 Hormone Replacement Therapy

Hormone Replacement Therapy (HRT) is the substitution of naturally occurring hormones in the human body with those that are manufactured. In the case of women that have had a hysterectomy we are considering oestrogen and possibly testosterone replacement therapy. When a woman has had a hysterectomy that removes her ovaries she will no longer produce oestrogen from her ovaries although she will continue to produce small amounts of oestrogen from the adrenal glands and fatty tissues[42,43]. However, this will not be enough to counteract the possible effects of oestrogen deficiency that we see begin with the onset of menopausal symptoms. If a woman has a hysterectomy that leaves her ovaries in place, she has a 50% chance of suffering ovarian failure within two - five years of surgery. This is not age dependent.

There are many things that women need to consider when they are faced with a surgical menopause and one of the major issues is whether or not to take HRT. It can be beneficial in alleviating the symptoms of the climacteric. Women should also consider the fact that they will be longer without the female sex hormones than their age related peers and that some of the natural protections that are offered by the sex hormones are lost, these include protection against heart disease and osteoporosis.

Some early studies have indicated that oestrogen supplementation in the form of HRT may also help to prevent the development of Alzheimer's Disease[44]. A study based in New York found that women who had taken oestrogen, after a natural menopause, for more than ten years were between 30-40% less likely to develop the disease than those women who had never taken HRT. The effects of HRT may be due to oestrogen regulating neurochemical transmitters and thus positively affecting neuronal atrophy[45].

There seems to be some consensus that women who have an early menopause through surgery should take HRT at least until the age that they would naturally have gone through the menopause, this is so that they reduce the risk of suffering from age related conditions earlier than they would have done. Women naturally produce oestrogen up to the age of the menopause and it would appear to be sensible to replace what would be there naturally. What a woman decides to do after the age of 50ish will be determined by considering the same factors that affect all women and will again be a matter of choice. At the very least, women who still have ovaries after surgery should have regular blood tests to check the amount of oestrogen they are producing so that they can make an informed choice. There seems to be little argument that HRT taken for up to ten years after a natural menopause does not adversely affect the body and there seems to be some evidence that women who do develop breast cancer have a better prognosis if they have taken HRT than if they had not[46], although this may of course be related to the type of cancer that they have.

Before deciding women should take into account a number of factors. These should include:

- whether there is a family history of osteoporosis
- whether she is in a high risk category related to osteoporosis

- whether there is a family history of heart disease
- whether she is in a high risk category related to heart disease
- whether she is worried about Alzheimer's disease
- whether she is suffering from severe climacteric symptoms

She may decide not to take HRT for some or all of the following reasons:

- if she has a history of breast cancer
- if there is a family history of breast cancer
- if she is in a high risk category related to breast cancer
- if she has a history of thrombosis
- if there is a family history of thrombosis
- if she is in a high risk category of thrombosis

1.5.1 Types Of Hormone Replacement Therapy

All HRT treatment for women that have had a hysterectomy consists of oestrogen only although a woman may also receive additional treatment to replace testosterone. When she begins taking HRT there may be some side effects such as possible weight gain, breast tenderness, headaches.

The usual method of administering HRT is to start with the lowest dose and to gradually increase it until the menopausal symptoms are relieved. However, this may not provide enough oestrogen to protect the bones and heart. Women that have their hysterectomies before the age of 40 will need more oestrogen as they will have been producing more before their operation.

Tablets

The most common way to administer HRT is by using tablets which must be taken every day. Tablets contain a larger amount of oestrogen as they will pass through the liver before being absorbed into the blood stream, the liver will inactivate 35-50% of the absorbed oestrogen, this is known as the first-pass effect[47]. It is also common for the blood oestrogen levels to fluctuate during the day, the levels of oestrogen being at their highest about 4 - 8 hours after taking the drug[48].

Patches

Patches are used on clean dry skin and placed on the buttocks or the lower abdomen. They are applied every three to four days and have few side effects other than skin irritation. They also have a habit of falling off when they get wet or in hot weather and can be embarrassing to use. As the oestrogen is not passing through the liver, much smaller doses can be used to achieve the same hormonal effects.

Implants

An implant of oestrogen is placed underneath the skin in the area of the abdomen. The implant is small, about the size of an apple pip, and it is inserted under local anaesthetic. This implant can last for up to six months and a woman will know when she needs to have another one because she will begin to experience some 'acute' menopausal symptoms, such as hot flushes and night sweats. The implant has advantages over other forms of administration as it avoids the liver, does not cause skin irritation as patches can and it can use smaller amounts of oestrogen than tablets need.

However, the implant is not without it's own possible side effect. Approximately 3% of implant users experience a syndrome called tachyphylaxis[49], which means that the dosage needs to be increased to obtain the same effect even though the levels of blood oestrogen are high enough. This usually happens when a new implant is inserted before the last one has finished completely. This side effect has led to claims that HRT is addictive.

Creams, Gels and Pessaries

Oestrogen Gel has recently been released in the UK although it has been used in Europe for some time. Oestrogen cream has been used for some time. The cream or gel is rubbed onto the skin of the upper arm or inner thigh every day, making sure it is fully absorbed. The irritation that may be experienced with patches is avoided with the creams and gels. Again smaller doses can be administered as the oestrogen is not passing through the liver first.

Pessaries are inserted high into the vagina and absorbed through the skin of the vagina into the blood stream as with creams and gels. Some women have reported an increase in libido when using pessaries and they do help to prevent vaginal dryness.

1.6 Oestrogen

Oestrogen is a powerful female sex hormone that regulates many aspects of women's lives. Initially it makes girls develop into women at puberty by stimulating breast growth, laying down fatty deposits, thickening the vagina and causing it to secrete mucous. It affects how the skin looks, whether bones are strong and healthy and it can protect against heart disease. It also regulates the menstrual cycle.

At the beginning of a woman's cycle about 30 egg follicles will start to ripen and produce oestrogen. When levels of oestrogen in the blood are highest the hypothalamus in the brain releases hormones that make a follicle release an egg.

Oestrogen can also affect the mood and it is thought that pre-menstrual syndrome, post-natal depression and menopausal depression are all caused by falling levels of oestrogen. According to John Studd, it is not the *amount* of oestrogen that affects the mood, but rather the fact that it is falling[50]. Exposure to oestrogen may also have an effect on the risk of developing breast cancer as it attaches itself to receptors in the breast on the surface of cells and stimulates them to divide in anticipation of producing milk and it is this division of cells that is thought to cause the risk.

There are at least three forms of oestrogen produced by the human body, Oestrone (E1), Oestradiol (E2) and Oestriol (E3)[51]. The first two oestrogen's, E1 and E2, are the most powerful they easily relieve menopausal symptoms and help the body stay healthy, however they may also be the cause of an increased risk of breast cancer and other side effects if they are given in high doses over a long period of time. The third form of oestrogen, E3 is made from a combination of E1 and E2 and is less potent. Therefore HRT made from E3 may be more appropriate for those women who are concerned about taking HRT for health reasons.

There is no standard as far as the production of oestrogen naturally is concerned. Women vary in their needs during their lifetime. When a woman has a hysterectomy that removes her ovaries, she will no longer produce oestrogen from them. She will continue to produce oestrogen in the adrenal gland and in fatty tissues but these are only very small amounts and are not enough even to prevent climacteric symptoms.

1.7 Testosterone

Although testosterone is a male hormone women still produce small amounts. Testosterone is produced by the ovaries and helps to regulate sex drive (libido), energy and mental state[52]. Following a natural menopause testosterone will continue to be produced by the ovaries in significant amounts for approximately twelve years[53]. Therefore a woman that has a surgical menopause that removes her ovaries will no longer produce testosterone and this may be responsible for the poor libido, depression and lack of energy that is often reported following surgery. Testosterone may also have a role to play in conserving bone after menopause and may be more suitable for women that are unable to take oestrogen supplements who have an increased risk of osteoporosis.

However testosterone should not be taken orally, in the form of tablets as it can damage the liver. The usual form of administration is by implant or by injection at regular intervals.

1.8 Thrombosis

As far as HRT is concerned, thrombosis refers to deep vein thrombosis. These are blood clots that can partially or completely block a blood vessel. The condition occurs most frequently in the legs but it can occur almost anywhere from the lower abdomen down. On average, deep vein thrombosis is fairly rare and affects about 1 person in 1700. People who are particularly susceptible are the elderly, those that are overweight and those who have a condition called polycythaemia (inability to control the rise in numbers of red blood cells)[54,55].

Deep vein thrombosis can also cause pulmonary embolism which is potentially fatal. A pulmonary embolism happens when pieces of a blood clot break away and becomes lodged in an artery in the lungs thus reducing the amount of oxygenated blood going to the heart.

The incidence of deep vein thrombosis appears to be increased by up to four times in HRT users and according to John Studd, the risk seems to be higher when treatment is first started and reduces significantly in long term users[56]. In a woman that is categorised as low risk, this may mean an increase of 1:5000. Any woman that already has a history of deep vein thrombosis or pulmonary embolism should avoid taking HRT, unless the thrombosis was as a result of surgery, accident, pregnancy or childbirth in which case there should not be an increased risk[57].

1.9 Breast Cancer

Perhaps the most significant worry about taking HRT is that of a possible increased risk of breast cancer. Breast cancer is an oestrogen dependent cancer and constitutes approximately 25% of all female cancers[58], therefore any woman who has an early menopause and does not take any oestrogen supplementation will actually reduce her risk of developing breast cancer in later life.

Currently, about one woman in thirteen will develop breast cancer before the age of 75 and if there is a family history (sister or mother with the disease) the risk is increased to one in eight[59]. Much of the initial data about the link with breast cancer and oestrogen supplementation has been taken from trials and studies based around the contraceptive pill. To date there have been over forty studies looking at the link between HRT and breast cancer and there has been no consensus about the results However, meta-analysis of the studies estimates that there is no increase in risk when HRT is taken for up to five to ten years. If the length of treatment is extended to fifteen years the increase appears to be about 25 - 30%[60].

Despite the worries over an increase in risk, it should be noted that these studies have taken place looking at women who had taken HRT following a *natural* menopause. Women who have an early surgical menopause would have naturally been producing oestrogen and its' supplementation is simply replacing what they would normally have.

Studies have also indicated that those women that do develop breast cancer whilst using HRT have a better prognosis and there is a decrease in the death rate compared to those that have not taken the supplements[61], however, this could be due to the fact that the women and their GP's are more aware and will be more vigilant about checking their breasts regularly.

Additional factors that women should take into account include:

- previous history of oestrogen dependent cancers
- family history of cancer
- starting menstruation before the age of eleven
- not having a child or having your first child after the age of 30
- being overweight
- women who have diets high in fat and low in fibre also have a higher levels of oestrogen in the blood

1.10 Alternatives To Hormone Replacement Therapy

1.10.1 Preventing Osteoporosis

Women can help to protect themselves against osteoporosis by taking HRT, however there may be some women who do not want to take it for many reasons. They may be in a high risk category for breast cancer or they may be at risk of thrombosis. Or they may not like taking drugs.

Calcium is vitally important in the health of the bones and extra calcium after the menopause may help to reduce the loss of bone that occurs. It is as important to get adequate amounts of Vitamin D as this is used by the body as a bone strengthener and allows the body to absorb calcium effectively. Vitamin D is usually made naturally by the body when it is exposed to sunlight and it can also be found in fish, egg yolks and cereals. A study in France has suggested that supplements of 800 units of Vitamin D3 and 1,200mg of Calcium had the effect of reducing fractures by 25%[62].

A woman should be getting at least 1,000mg of calcium per day, although a joint study by the office of Population and Census, MAFF and the Department of Health in the UK; in 1990 showed that the average daily intakes for women had fallen to 730mg[63]. There are many foods that are very rich in calcium although those that are none dairy contain calcium that is less easily absorbed than the calcium obtained from milk, fish, hard cheeses and yoghurt.

There are also a number of treatments for osteoporosis. They include Calcitonin supplementation, Biophosphonates and Anabolic Steroids.

Calcitonins are hormones that are naturally produced by the thyroid gland and work by stopping bone loss by blocking the actions of osteoclasts, the cells that break bone down. At present they are available for treatment with injection and nasal spray (the nasal spray has not yet been approved in the UK).

Biophosphonates inhibit bone loss by attaching themselves to the bone and preventing the osteoclasts from working effectively. They are available as tablets under the name "etidronate" and have been used to treat both Paget's disease and spinal osteoporosis.

Anabolic Steroids have been used to build up muscle and bone mass, they are used only with caution as they can cause women to become more masculine with long term use (over three years) and can also increase the risk of heart disease and extreme fluid retention.

1.10.2 Preventing Heart Disease

Arterial disease such as heart disease and stroke are the most common causes of death amongst post-menopausal women in the UK. In 1987 in England and Wales approximately 65,000 women died from heart disease and 45,000 from stoke. Compare this with the 18,000 deaths from breast cancer and the risk can be put into perspective.

It is essential that if a woman is unable or unwilling to take HRT that she reduces any risks by stopping smoking, reducing weight, and taking exercise. Taking care with diet is also important and there is some evidence that increasing the intake of calcium can help to lower blood pressure.

The vitamins A, C and E are known as the anti-oxidant vitamins and play a key role in helping to keep the heart healthy. They help to reduce damage to the blood vessels by free radicals. Vitamin E also reduces damage to the 'good' LDL (lower density lipoprotein) cholesterol. Recommended daily intakes by Dr Sandra Cabot are:

- 20 mgs of beta-carotene (Vitamin A),
- 4,000 milligrams of Vitamin C,
- 100 - 500 international units of Vitamin E[64].

1.10.3 Natural Plant Oestrogen's

There are over 300 plants that have oestrogen's in them and if they are consumed regularly enough they can have a mild oestrogenic effect on women[65]. The most potent of the plant oestrogen's is Coumestrol even though it is about 200 times weaker than human oestrogen. Because the plant oestrogen's have such a mild effect the side effects found with conventional HRT should be avoided.

Other good sources of natural oestrogen's are soya beans, soybean sprouts and crushed linseeds. The diet can be varied by including apples, beets, cabbage, carrots, chickpeas, cucumbers, green beans, oats, olives, parsley, potatoes. rhubarb, rice, sesame seeds and sunflower seeds.

1.10.4 Other Dietary Supplements

Supplements that are particularly useful for women going through the menopause can help protect against some of the dangers of oestrogen deficiency and can also help to relieve some of the more unpleasant symptoms. They include nutritional therapies, vitamins, essential fatty acids, minerals and amino acids.

There are special formulations to help prevent osteoporosis that contain calcium and vitamin D together with other minerals. A good multivitamin supplement can also help to maintain healthy levels of all body nutrients. Vitamin B6 has been recommended for women that have pre-menstrual syndrome and is also useful for women going through the menopause since both of these conditions are caused by the same hormone. Essential fatty acids can be obtained from starflower and evening primrose oil supplements.

Here's Health magazine published four steps to a natural menopause[66]. It includes:

- reducing stress as this affects the endocrine system that controls hormone balance, blood sugar levels, energy levels and calcium balance;
- using essential fatty acids so that the body can produce prostaglandin's to help maintain a healthy hormone balance;
- vitamin and mineral supplementation particularly of vitamin C, B3, B6, zinc and magnesium, again this combination will help to maintain healthy hormone balances;
- general healthy lifestyle with eating well and exercising regularly.

References

1. **Khastgir, G. and J. Studd.** *Hysterectomy and HRT.* in press.
2. **Womens Health.** *Hysterectomy*. Women's Health, London. 1995 p.1.
3. **Khastgir, G. and J. Studd.** ref. 1.
4. Ibid
5. **Smith, Dr T.**(ed). *The New Macmillan Guide to Family Health.* Macmillan, London. 1989. p.615.
6. **Womens Health.** ref. 2. p.2.

7. Ibid

8. **Smith, Dr T.**(ed). ref.5. p.615.

9. Ibid

10. **Khastgir, G. and J. Studd.** ref. 1.

11. **Helstrom, L. et al.** *Sexuality after hysterectomy; a factor analysis of women's sexual lives before and after hysterectomy*. Obstetric Gynaecology 81. 1993. p.p.357-362.

12. **Cabot, Dr S.** *The Menopause Handbook*. Boxtree Limited, London. 1996. p.p.187-190.

13. **Khastgir, G. and J. Studd.** ref. 1.

14. **Cabot, Dr S.** ref. 12. p.93.

15. Ibid. p.13.

16. Ibid

17. **Women's Health.** *The Menopause*. Women's Health, London. 1995. p.1.

18. Ibid

19. **Wilson, Dr R.C.D.** *Understanding HRT and the Menopause*. Consumers Association Ltd, London. 1992. p.27.

20. **Cabot, Dr S**. ref. 12. p.17.

21. **Smith, Dr T.** (ed). ref. 5. p.560.

22. **Kaplin, Dr F.S.** *Osteoporosis, Pathophysiology and Prevention*. Clinical Symposia, 39(1). 1987. p.p.1-32.

23. **Dover, C**. *Ward Lock Family Health Guide - Osteoporosis*. Ward Lock, London. 1994. p.7.

24. Ibid. p.10.

25. **Cabot, Dr S.** ref. 12. p.28.

26. **Hampson, A.** *Brittle Words: The impact of health information on patients compliance with treatment*. M.A. Dissertation. Department of Information and Library Studies, Loughborough University of Technology. 1995. p.41.

27. **Khastgir, G. and J. Studd.** ref. 1.

28. **Rees, A.M.**(ed). *Osteoporosis*. Consumer Health USA. Oryx Press; Phoenix. 1995. p.p.434-436.

29. **Cabot, Dr S.** ref. 12. p.p.30-48.

30. **Hampson, A.** ref. 26. p.p.40-45.

31. **Cabot, Dr S.** ref. 12. p.34.

32. **Effectiveness Review Bulletin,** *Osteoporosis*. Bandolier. (URL: http://www.jr2.ox.ac.uk:80/Bandolier/band3/b3-4.html), 07/02/97, 18/02/97.

33. **Effectiveness Review Bulletin,** *Osteoporosis*. Bandolier. (URL: http://www.jr2.ox.ac.uk:80/Bandolier/band3/b3-4.html), 07/02/97, 18/02/97.

34. **Cabot, Dr S.** ref. 12. p.25.

35. **Dover, C.** ref. 23. p.33.

36. **Cabot, Dr S.** ref. 12. p.26.

37. **Khastgir, G. and J. Studd.** ref. 1.

38. **Stamphner, M.J.** et. al. *Post Menopausal Estrogen Therapy and Cardiovascular Disease.* New England Journal of Medicine, 325(11). 1991. p.p.76-62

39. **Cabot, Dr S.** ref. 12. p.26.

40. **Bailey, J.** *HRT and Cardio-Protection: Unravelling the Tangled Web.* European Menopause Journal Symposium Report. (URL: http://www.medscape.com/PMSI/EMJ/1..01.05.bailey/em0401.05.bailey.html), 6/11/96, 14/05/97.

41. **Womens Health.** *HRT.* Women's Health, London. 1996. p.1.

42. **Wilson, Dr R.** ref. 19. p.19.

43. **Boulton A.** *Hormone Therapy may protect against Alzheimer's Disease.* British Medical Journal 313. p442.

44. **Tang, M.X. et. al.** *Effect of oestrogen during menopause on risk and age at onset of Alzheimer's disease.* The Lancet, 348. p.p.429-432.

45. **Khastgir, G. and J. Studd.** ref. 1.

46. Ibid

47. Ibid

48. Ibid

49. **Cabot, Dr S.** ref. 12. p.75.

50. **Khastgir, G. and J. Studd.** ref. 1.

51. Ibid

52. **Cabot, Dr S.** ref. 12. p.13.

53. **Smith, Dr T.**(ed). ref. 5. p.416.

54. Ibid. p.440.

55. **Khastgir, G.and J. Studd.** ref. 1.

56. Ibid

57. **European Menopause Journal Symposium Report.** *State of the Art Practical HRT*. EMJ, 3(2). 1996. p.p.71-73. (URL: http://www.medscape.com/PMSI/EMJ/1...6.kenemans/em0302.06.kenemans.html), 20/02/97.

58. **Cabot, Dr S.** ref. 12. p.109.

59. **Khastgir, G. and J. Studd.** ref. 1.

60. **Cabot, Dr S.** ref.12. p.110.

61. **Dover, C.** ref. 23. p.43.

62. Ibid. p.51.

63. **Cabot, Dr S.** ref. 12. p.153.

64. **Setchell, K.D.R.** *Non steroidal estrogens of dietary origin: Possible roles in Hormone Dependent Disease*. American Journal of Clinical Nutrition, 40. p.p.569-78.

65. **Cabot, Dr S.** ref 12. p.155.

66. **Holford, P**. *Be healthy, be happy without HRT*. Here's Health, March 1995 p.p.18-22.

2. Current Sources Of Information For Hysterectomy Patients

Even as far back as 1979 there was considerable research that indicated that patients would like more information about any medical condition they may have, the treatments available and it's management[1]. This requirement is likely to have increased rather than decreased, particularly with the introduction of the Patient Charter in 1991.

Patients may be given information, but they are often given it verbally and not in a formal written format and they may go on to forget it within 5 minutes of hearing it[2]. This could be due to shock at news not expected or the patients inability to understand what has been said or even the professional's poor explanation.

The Audit Commission has found that a number of patients had not been given adequate information about their condition, care and any alternative forms of treatment. The reasons for this they suggested, were possibly:

- "failure on the part of staff to provide information" for a number of reasons, possibly beyond the control of staff,
- information not being easy to understand,
- patient misconceptions about physiology not being corrected by professionals,
- limitations of memory,
- patient diffidence,

- assumptions on the part of professionals that patients do not want information[3].

The provision of adequate information in a non-verbal format allows the patient to read, watch or listen to it in their own time. They can then assess their own needs for further information on a less emotional level. Andrew Hampson has offered evidence to suggest that adequate information improves a patient's compliance with their treatment as they feel they are part of the process that is managing their health[4]. He also goes on to suggest that some people also use the health information they receive to assess any risk factors that may be inherent in the treatment and if they feel that the risk factors are too great they will not comply with the treatment, this applies particularly to prescribed drugs. He goes on to say

> *"Patients are using information to make informed decisions about treatments they are prescribed. The ability to make such choices suggests that information has empowered individuals, leaving the decision to comply with treatment in their hands"* [5].

A study of hysterectomy patients in Bath has found that, contrary to some beliefs on the part of the medical profession, giving patients information does not have a detrimental effect on them, rather it has confirmed that those patients that had appropriate information prior to the operation, either verbally or written, experienced less pre-operative anxiety and less post-operative vomiting, they were discharged earlier and were walking outside the house earlier than the control group used who had professional attention only[6]. Other research has also found that forthright and realistic information has not increased patient's fears over their hysterectomy, rather it has resulted in an increase in patient participation in their health management[7].

The study at Bath has also found that most hysterectomy patients want information and the most popular type of information required during the early 80's was about the physical effects of the surgery and patients wanted this before the surgery took place[8]. However, it has also been shown that if a patient has been offered additional information to that received about the physical effects of surgery, for instance covering physical and psychological issues, that this is preferred by patients[9]. Research has also shown that there is a need for social support following hysterectomy, due mainly to the physical limitations, imposed by surgery, on discharge from hospital. Where women have been given this information prior to surgery it was found that they were better able to cope and had fewer post-hysterectomy complications than other patients at the six week check-up.

There are of course other issues that increase the understanding and compliance of patients undergoing hysterectomy, not least of these is having access to information about the most commonly prescribed post-hysterectomy treatment, Hormone Replacement Therapy (HRT). As Chapter 1 has shown there are long term benefits to be obtained from taking HRT, but overall it is estimated that only 12 - 16% of patients in the UK that could take the treatment are doing so. Compliance with the treatment has been shown to be improved with "appropriate and adequate counselling", this includes receiving information that is suitable[10]. Many studies have shown that women link HRT to a risk of breast cancer and to thrombosis, these are issues not very well understood and the appropriateness of the treatment can be dismissed in the light of such fears if not put into perspective with adequate and timely information that allows a woman to make an *informed* decision.

2.1 Recognised Traditional Sources Of Information

The types of information that women may receive from their GP or hospital about hysterectomy and/or HRT includes:

- Leaflets or instructions from the hospital (appendix 1) which generally provide details about the operation and what a patient should expect before and after their stay in hospital
- Health Education authority leaflets on the menopause.
- Leaflets and booklets about the menopause and hormone replacement therapy from the pharmaceutical companies producing the drugs, these include leaflets about particular drugs and also about conditions such as osteoporosis.

Typically the information consists of two distinct types:

- leaflets about the surgery and it's physical effects
- leaflets about the menopause and/or HRT

Much of the information about hysterectomy discusses the issues of surgery and it's physical effects and it tends not to consider the implications of the menopause for a woman that has had a hysterectomy. The information given about the menopause and hormone replacement therapy looks at it from the perspective of the woman who has a natural menopause and is not directed towards those having a hysterectomy. In the light of this vast difference in emphasis, it is entirely possible that women may not be made aware of some the major implications of their surgery. They may for instance assume that they will not have a menopause if they are too young to have it naturally, they may not be aware of the effects of testosterone on their bodies or of the implications for their heart.

The majority of information that is provided for women about HRT is found either in leaflets that are in the prescription box, or leaflets available free of charge at the surgery or hospital about related conditions such as osteoporosis. Despite the fact that in the main these leaflets are produced though sponsorship by the major drug companies and are therefore biased, they also provide information from the point of view of women going through the menopause naturally and are not completely relevant for hysterectomised women.

2.2 Additional Sources Of Information

There are many other information sources for women having a hysterectomy. They include support organisations, Regional Health Information services, books and magazines and the Internet. However a woman may not be aware of them unless she has already obtained additional information herself or from her GP.

2.2.1 Support Organisations

The support organisations include The Amarant Trust, The Menopause Society, The National Osteoporosis Society and Women's Health. These four represent the most appropriate for women having a hysterectomy although there are many more that may offer some support and additional information. A complete list is contained in Appendix 2. There was also the Hysterectomy Support Network but it was disbanded in 1996.

The Amarant Trust; is an organisation set up to "promote a better understanding of the menopause and greater awareness of the benefits of Hormone Replacement Therapy"[11]. The Trust provides a number of information services, these include 0891 24 hour telephone information lines and 'Friends of the Amarant Trust' also receive regular newsletters and a direct telephone line to a Menopause Health Counsellor.

The National Osteoporosis Society is a charitable organisation "dedicated to working towards eradicating this preventable disease, funding research programmes and ensuring all sufferers can obtain appropriate advice and treatment"[12]. It produces a number of leaflets and booklets with a relevance to hysterectomy, including information about hysterectomy and osteoporosis, HRT and breast cancer and diet and bone health. Members also receive quarterly newsletters and access to the local group network.

The British Menopause Society supports the advancement of knowledge, interest and study of all matters connected with the menopause; to provide high standards of training for those involved in advising women

Women's Health is a charity "committed to providing information from a women's centred perspective, to enable women to make informed decisions about their health"[13]. Women can obtain information leaflets about a variety of subjects related to hysterectomy and members also receive a quarterly newsletter.

2.2.2 Regional Health Information Services

There are a number of regional health information services providing health information that are funded mainly by the local health authorities. They were set up as a requirement of the Patients Charter, to "provide information to the public to empower them to become more active in relation to their own health"[14]. Any member of the public can contact them either by telephone, by writing to them or by visiting them and they can request information on health subjects that interest them. However the services provided vary greatly depending on what information resources they have access to.

2.2.3 Books And Magazines

There are many books either available to buy or through the local library. Those used in this study are detailed in the bibliography. However, many of the books are aimed at those women going through a natural menopause and the information given about hysterectomy is often incidental and may assume that the physical responses of women having a surgical menopause will be the same as those of a woman having a natural menopause. The books considering HRT again tend to consider the subject from the point of view of a woman going though the menopause naturally and any information specifically for women who have had a hysterectomy tends to be more incidental than deliberate.

A list of books currently in print for women that have had a hysterectomy can be found in Appendix 4. This list is specific to the UK only. These books include information about the operation and what to expect physically, but on the whole do not provide very much information about the menopause, HRT or alternative health treatments.

There are also a number of specific health magazines available in the UK. A list is included in Appendix 4. The subjects covered in these magazines are many and varied and are often a major source of information for women. It would be fair to say that not all of the information is properly referenced and sourced and there is often a great deal of bias. This type of information has led to many of the claims that have been made about HRT being addictive or causing breast cancer.

2.2.4 Internet Resources

Health information on the Internet is one of the largest subject areas in this rapidly growing media. For anyone that has access to the Internet it is becoming easy to locate information about very specific subjects and the level of currency is often greater than can be obtained from more traditional sources of information. Despite this, the number of resources that are related specifically to the subject of hysterectomy are few and consist of support networks, with mailing lists that patients can write to, commercial information supporting new methods of operation or drugs and single pages within general medical sites (the latter are usually within electronic journals and are sources of peer reviewed information for the medical profession). A list of these sites is contained in Appendix 5.

There are a greater number of sites about related information such as osteoporosis, heart disease and hormone replacement therapy although as with the information contained in printed sources it is sometimes difficult to extract the relevant pieces.

Although there is information available on the Internet there are a number of considerations that patients must take into account before relying on it to make a decision that affects their health:

- the information may be based on the current practice of another country which may not apply within the UK.
- the information may not be up to date.
- it may be difficult to locate quality information, and the use of subject gateways may be advisable.
- information may not be provided for the consumer, but be for the medical profession and as such may be difficult to understand by the patient.
- information that is provided outside the UK, usually America, will mean that all contact information and support networks will be with regard to the country of origin.

The most important area of concern however, is the fact that anyone can publish information on the Internet and it may be wise to consider information as "personal opinion" if it is not referenced and/or supported as there is very little editorial control of content. It would be reasonable, however, to assume that information provided by, say, the large medical journals or site such as the BMJ and Medscape is a good resource. Taking this as a basic assumption, there are those patients that have had to learn about their condition due to lack of medical information from the professionals and in some senses can be seen as more expert than the experts.

A difficulty when attempting to justify publishing health information on the Internet is it's lack of accessibility. According to William's there were approximately 100,000 people with access to the Internet in the UK in 1995[15]. Although the Internet is still in it's infancy this figure has probably increased dramatically in the intervening time.

REFERENCES

1. **Ley P.** *Improving clinical communication*. In: Oborne, D. Gruneberg, M.M. Euer, J.R.. Research in Psycology and Medicine. Academic Press, London. 1997.

2. **Ley, P. and P.W. Bradshaw, D. Eaves, C.M. Walker.** *A method for increasing patients recall of information presented by Doctors*. Psychological Medicine, 3. p.p.217-220.

3. **Audit Commission**. *What seems to be the matter? the communication between hospitals and patients*. H.M.S.O. 1993.

4. **Hampson, A.** Brittle Words, *The Impact of Health Information on Patient's Compliance with Treatment*. M.A. Dissertation, Department of Information and Library Studies, Loughborough University of Technology. 1995; p.112.

5. Ibid

6. Ibid. p.113.

7. **Young, L. and M. Humphrey.** *Cognitive Methods of preparing women for hysterectomy: Does a booklet help?.* British Journal of Clinical Psychology, 24. 1985. p.p.303-314.

8. **Deny M.** *Informed consent, emotional responses of patients. Postgraduate Medicine,* 60(5). 1975. p.p.205-209.

9. **Scriven, A.** *Information needs of hysterectomy patients.* Nursing Standard, 9. 1994.

10. Ibid

11. **Okon, M.A. and S. Lee, T.C. Li.** *A Study to Examine Women's Knowledge, Perception and Acceptability of Hormone Replacement Therapy.* European Menopause Journal, 3 (2). 1996 p.p.47-52. (URL: http://www.medscape.com/PMSI/EMJ/1...em0302.02.okon/em03 02.02.okon.html) 20/02/97.

12. **Amarant Trust.** *Information Leaflet.* The Amarant Trust. 1997.

13. **National Osteoporosis Society.** *You've had a hysterectomy.* National Osteoporosis Society, London. 1996.

14. Women's Health to Linda Newall, 20 May 1997.

15. **Williams, G.** *Using the Internet to attract inward investment and tourism.* Electronic Public Information Provision, Fifth Annual Seminar, Loughborough University of Technology. September 1995.

3. Research Focus

The study was conducted over a six month period, February - September 1997. There were no control groups used because of the short time frame and due to the fact that the study was attempting only to document current practice and identify possible areas for change rather than to actually initiate the change itself.

Postal questionnaires were used as a survey technique to gather quantitative data (Appendix 10 and 11). This technique allows for a consistent format to be maintained, helps to ensure a reduction in bias and allows the collection of large amounts of data in shorter periods of time. Respondents could ensure their anonymity and may thus be more likely to respond to the questions honestly. As the respondents were dispersed geographically, the data could be gathered at minimum cost.

3.1 Sample Population

Initially, it was intended that the sample population would be drawn from the patient lists of General Practitioner's. They would be women who had had a hysterectomy preferably before the age of 50. The number of GP's that responded to the initial call for participation was low (two replied), a second method of contacting GP's that were interested was through EMIS, who published an article outlining the research proposal and asking for participation[1]. This did not produce any GP's willing to take part. Support organisations (see appendix two) were then contacted to see if they would be willing/able to participate and one replied positively (Women's Health[2]) providing the names and addresses of patients willing to be contacted by researchers. Finally popular magazines were contacted with a request to print a letter seeking participation by patients and GP's.

3.2 Data Collection - Patients

A discussion list hosted by Mailbase called gp-uk[3], was contacted and an introductory message was posted to the group explaining the outline of the project, some of the background and details of some of the issues thought to be important at that stage. A total of ten replies to the initial message were received. A second message was posted to clarify some of the points from the initial message. From the second message there were six replies.

Following this initial contact, a third email was sent to the 16 people that had replied positively to either the first or second message asking whether they would take part in the survey and explaining what form of support was required. Two GP's responded to this message and agreed to take questionnaires on behalf of patients.

Louise Simpson of the EMIS National User Group also replied and offered to publish details of the project in a future issue of their journal[4]. EMIS is a computer records system used by approximately 75% of GP's in the UK. It was hoped that this would allow other GP's to participate in the study if they had not been aware of the postings on gp-uk.

Twenty questionnaires were sent to Dr Ruth Livingstone and twenty were sent to Dr Mike Corfield. It was clear at this point that there was no further interest from GP's, and alternative sources of women willing to complete questionnaires was sought.

Letters were sent to organisations supporting women's health information, requesting help (appendix six). Replies were received from all but one, the Margaret Pyke Centre, which appears to have been either disbanded or has moved. One organisation, Women's Health sent contact details for a total of twenty seven women who had said they were willing to be contacted by researchers. Questionnaires and a covering letter (appendix seven) were sent out to the twenty seven women.

Finally, popular magazines (appendix eight) that have a letter page were also contacted asking for the letter to be published. To date a letter has been published in Here's Health[5]. The covering letter sent to women who responded to Here's Health is contained in Appendix nine.

Questionnaires were also sent to women who requested them from the researcher personally. They were women who had heard about the study from others and wanted to take part.

In order to improve the response rate to the questionnaires a covering letter explaining a little of the project and a stamped addressed envelope were also sent. The questionnaires had a return date of 31st May or 31st July, depending upon the original source.

3.3 Data Collection - GP's

The collection of data from the GP's was managed in the same way as for patients.

Two questionnaires were sent to Dr Ruth Livingstone and five were sent to Dr Mike Corfield. A GP in Swadlincote, South Derbyshire agreed to allow questionnaires be sent to other Doctors in the practice and six were sent.

The letter's sent to support organisations and the popular press have all stated that both patients and GP's were required for the study.

3.4 Questionnaire Design - Patients

Twenty three closed questions were used to ease the collection of the data and its' subsequent analysis. This also reduced the opportunity for ambiguous answers. Of the twenty three questions, nine were multiple response, three had an "other" choice that allowed patients to define the answer more clearly and three questions relating to the operation and the information given at that time had a "don't know" section for those women that were less sure. The questionnaire was designed to consider five areas of understanding:

General Health Information. Whether patient information was available and if so what type it was. If there was patient information available for other medical conditions this should produce some positive responses from patients who had had a hysterectomy. (Questions three and four).

Hysterectomy Information. What the patient had received and understood about the operation they had had, this would also be a good indicator of the amount of information that they had received, even if they were not aware of it. (Questions five to 11).

HRT Information. What the patient had received and understood about Hormone Replacement Therapy and the issues surrounding it. (Questions 12 to 19).

Use of Alternative Sources of Information. Whether the patient needed to or was interested enough to seek out information for themselves to supplement what they had been given. (Questions 20 and 21).

Information Patients Feel They Need. What information the patient felt she needed, this area should give good indicators again of what the patient understands about her medical condition. (Questions 22 and 23).

The information gained from the five areas would then be used to create two information resources based upon the analysis of the answers.

All questionnaires were accompanied by a covering letter from either the GP or the researcher. This was used to introduce the study and reassured the patients that the questionnaires would all be analysed anonymously.

The method of analysis was through SPSS, a windows based statistical package used in the Department of Information and Library Studies, and Excel. All questionnaires were coded with an identifier for the source (GP, Magazine etc...) and a unique number. All of the questions were either single or multiple response and the patient was directed to tick those that applied to her. There were also sections that allowed the patient to make their own response such the brand of Hormone Replacement Therapy that they might be taking. Finally, the patient was invited to make comments and to indicate if they would like to see any results at the end of the study. If the patients had access to the WWW and wanted to review the web site they were asked to leave an email address so that they could be contacted when the site was on-line.

3.5 Questionnaire Design - GP's

Nineteen closed questions were used to ease the collection of the data and its' subsequent analysis. This also reduced the opportunity for ambiguous answers. Of the nineteen questions, eight were multiple choice, seven had an "other" choice that allowed GP's to define the answer more clearly and two questions relating to the information given to patients had a "don't know" section for GP's that were less sure. The questionnaire was designed to consider five elements:

- The type of health information currently provided by the practice.
- Reasons and types of hysterectomy, to see if there were any common reasons and ways of dealing with medical problems.
- How the GP's viewed the information given to patients, ie where the patients get it from, who gives it to them, what types they are given. The GP's were invited to comment on whether they thought the information was effective.
- What they felt about alternative sources of information.
- What they felt were the issues that their patients were most concerned with.

All of these areas were to be considered against the reactions from patients that responded from the surgeries that took part to see if there was a difference between the patient and GP points of view.

The method of analysis was to be through SPSS and Excel. All questionnaires were coded with two codes, an identifier for the source (Practice, Magazine etc...) and a unique number. All the questions were single/multiple choice and the GP was directed to tick those that applied to their practice. There were also sections that allowed the GP to be more specific. Finally, the GP was invited to make comments and to indicate if they would like to see any results at the end of the study. If the GP's had access to the WWW and wanted to review the web site they were asked to leave an email address so that they could be contacted when the site was on-line.

3.6 Method Of Data Analysis

A total of 65 questionnaires were returned by patients, of these 62 were analysed through SPSS and Excel. Three were returned too late to be used.

Each of the questions were analysed separately and those questions that had the possibility of multiple answers were analysed by separate answer. The multiple answer questions were then analysed by Excel to produce quantitative charts across the whole question.

The questionnaires sent to GP's were not analysed. Of the 13 questionnaires sent out only three were returned and it was not considered to be an adequate sample.

REFERENCES

1. **E.M.I.S National User Group,** Sutton Place, 49 Stoney Street, The Lace Market, Nottingham, NG1 1LX. Louise Simpson to Linda Newall. email. 11/02/97
2. **Women's Health Organisation**. London, 1997.
3. **gp-uk discussion list.** (URL: http://www.mailbase.ac.uk/lists/gp-uk/), 18/08/97.
4. Louise Simpson to Linda Newall. email. 11/02/97
5. **Newall, L.** *Informed Choice*. Here's Health. July 1997. p.7.

4. Results

4.1 Problems Encountered When Analysing The Data

The main problems encountered were respondents that had made more than one response to those questions that required only a single response, or when they had made no response at all. In these circumstances the replies given were recorded as void and were not marked. All percentages are to the nearest full percent.

The results are analysed under the following seven headings:

1. Response to Questionnaire
2. Age of Respondent
3. General Health Information
4. Hysterectomy Information
5. Hormone Replacement Therapy Information
6. Alternative Sources of Information Used
7. Information Women Would Like to Receive

4.2 Response To Questionnaire

A total of 88 questionnaires were sent out. These can be broken down into the following groupings: 20 were sent to each of two GP surgery's (Stamford and Wokingham), 26 were sent to members of Women's Health, eight were sent to women personally requesting the form and 14 were sent to women who followed up the letter to Here's Health. Of the 88 sent out, 65 were returned, representing a return rate of 73.86%. The percentage returns for each grouping were; Stamford Surgery - 15 replies (75%), Wokingham Surgery - four replies (20%), Women's Health - 24 replies (92.3%), Personal requests - eight replies (100%), Here's Health - 14 replies (100%).

Only 62 questionnaires were analysed as three were returned after the final date of 31 July 1997.

4.3 Age Of Respondent

Of the women that were analysed one (1.6%) reply came from a woman that was in the 20-30 years of age category, 15 replies (24.2%) came from women that were in the 30-40 years of age category, 26 replies (41.9%) came from women in the 40-50 years of age category and 16 replies (25.8%) came from women that were over 50 years of age.

4.4 General Health Information

Figures one and two show that the most popular forms of health information available from the surgery were dietary advice (53%) and information on particular conditions/diseases (47%). However, despite this greater numbers of women said that they did not have access to any information in all subjects apart from dietary advice.

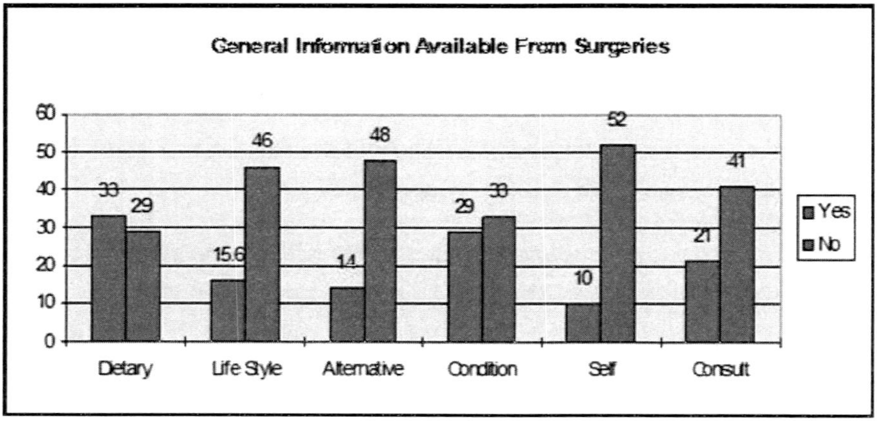

Figure 1

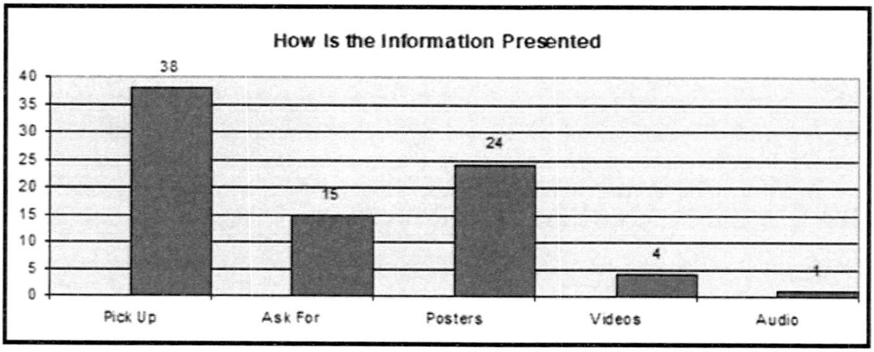

Figure 2

Information is usually presented in the form of leaflets that the patients can collect themselves (61%), or on posters that are around the surgery (39%). Four women did report having access to videos and one reported access to audio material.

4.5 Hysterectomy

The most common type of hysterectomy reported by women is a 'total hysterectomy with bilateral oopherectomy', removing uterus, fallopian tubes, ovaries and cervix (61% of respondents). Only one woman reported having a different type of hysterectomy, a wertheim's hysterectomy where part of other abdominal organs are removed at the same time. One woman reported having two separate operations, the first to remove uterus and cervix and the second to remove the ovaries and fallopian tubes. One woman did not complete the question.

The most common reason for having a hysterectomy was reported as fibroids by 29% of respondents. 21% of respondents reported endometriosis as the cause and 14.5% of respondents said heavy bleeding was the reason for their surgery. This seems to follow the national trend which shows that hysterectomy is an elective procedure and is rarely performed for saving life[1]. Only 13% of respondents reported cancer as the reason for their hysterectomy (uterine - one case, ovarian - three cases and cervical - four cases). Four respondents used two criteria, heavy bleeding and fibroids or endometriosis, these were marked as unknown although one of the main symptoms for each of these conditions is heavy bleeding.

The information that respondents received at the time of surgery is shown in Figure three and shows that the most common information received concerned the surgical procedure, 40% reported receiving information about HRT when they had their hysterectomy, although eight women (13%) reported receiving no information at all.

66% of the respondents reported that the information they had received was easy to understand, although nine women (14.5%) did not complete the question. 74% of women reported that they saw their GP about their operation one to three times, and seven women (11%) reported not having to see their GP to discuss their operation at all. 51% of the respondents said that questions they asked were answered fully 'most of the time', 27% reported their questions were answered fully 'some of the time', 14% reported that they were not happy with the answers they had received and four women (10%) declined to answer the question or marked more than one answer. 37% of the respondents reported that they had felt fully prepared for their surgery, although 59% said that they were only partly ready for surgery or that they were not at all prepared.

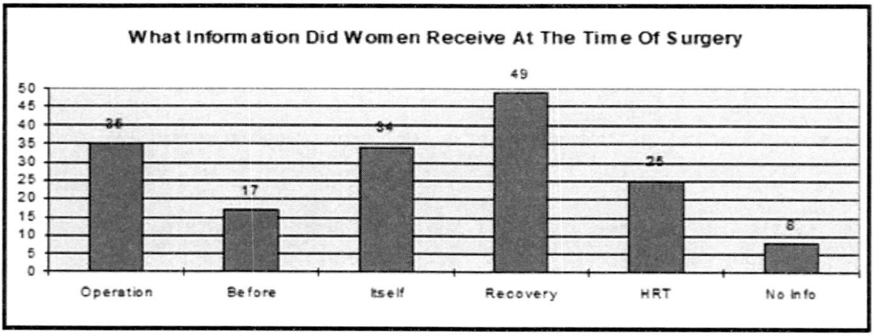

Figure 3

4.6 Hormone Replacement Therapy

The most common information received by respondents concerned osteoporosis and no-one reported having received any information at all about alternatives to HRT. 38 women (61%) reported that they had not received any information about HRT from their GP and 34 (55%) reported that they had not received it from their consultant. This question also produced ambiguous results as the researcher cannot be sure whether women had received information from either the GP or the Consultant or from neither.

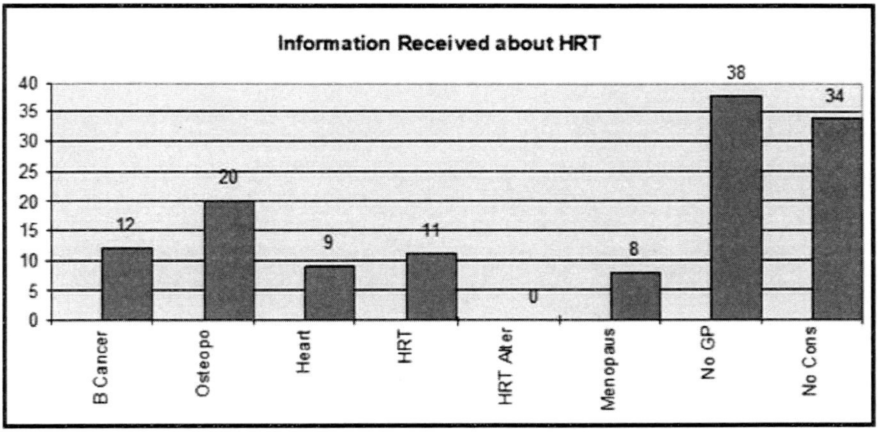

Figure 4

Respondents reported that they received most of the information about HRT from either their Consultant (19%) or GP (18%), although 43% had said that they had received no information at all (see Figure three). There were a number of discrepancies in the answers between the questions that asked patients to say whether they had received information on HRT. This will be discussed in the next chapter.

Women also said that the most common time to receive information about HRT was following the operation (39%), this could have been either immediately following surgery or many months after and from the comments of some women was only received when they actually asked for it. 35% of the women also reported that they had not received any information about HRT from any healthcare professional.

The type of information that was most commonly received was leaflets produced by the hospital or doctor, with 24% of women reporting this, although 39% said they had not been given any information at all.

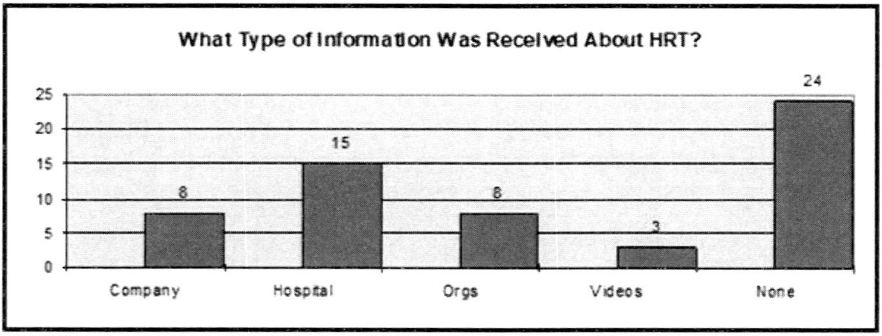

Figure 5

61% of women reported that they were currently taking HRT, although two women (3%) said that the type was an alternative form, progesterone cream, that is not available on prescription. These two answers were recorded as positive.

The most common type of HRT being used by women that said they were taking it was tablets (66%), patches were the next most common with respondents (18%). The women taking HRT reported that the most common type of information that they were given about HRT was drug company leaflets (66%), possibly those within the prescription boxes, although 18% reported having been given no information at all.

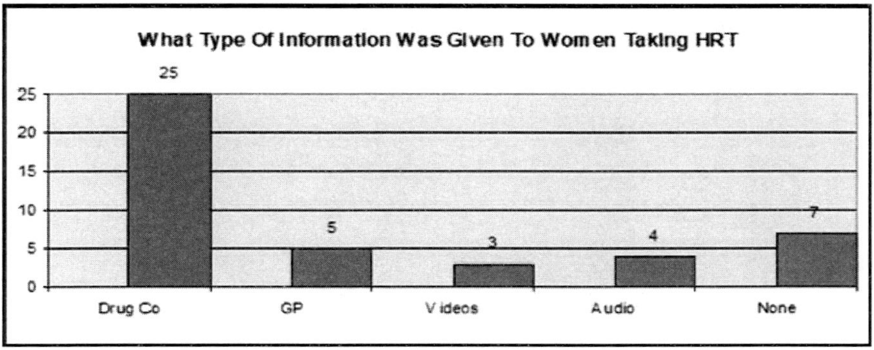

Figure 6

4.7 Additional Information Used

Figure seven shows that 84% of the respondents did use other sources of information to supplement what they had received from healthcare professionals. 52% of women recorded that the source used most was the media this included magazines, newspapers and television. 42% of women said that they had contacted support organisations, 37% said that they had got information from friends and 27% said that they had used the library as a source of information. Most women that said they had used additional sources of information used more than one source of information although 16% did report not using any other sources of information.

The support organisations listed in the questionnaire were only a limited sample of those available. 13% of women said that they had heard of The Menopause Society, 36% said that they had heard of the Hysterectomy Support Network, but only a small number pointed out that it was now disbanded, and 40% reported that they had heard of the National Osteoporosis Society.

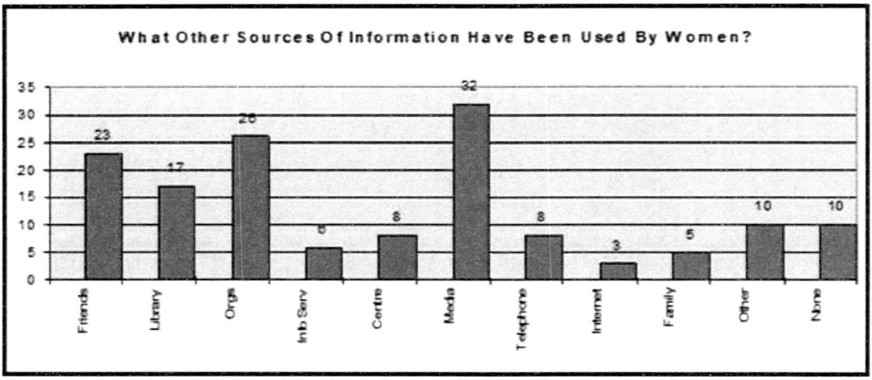

Figure 7

4.8 Information The Patient Needs

Women most commonly reported that the information they would like more of was about alternatives to HRT (61%) and the information that they would least need was on hysterectomy (26%). The former reply bears out the answers to question 12 where no-one reported receiving information about alternatives to HRT. The women responding to the questionnaire are all post-surgery and would not feel that they had a need for information about hysterectomy now.

Women felt that the most appropriate place to be able to get information would be through their GP's surgery (58%), although 31% did mark more than one answer implying that they would like to have a choice of information services. Five percent of women reported having obtained additional information from the Internet, although only 2% reported that they would like to receive the most information from the Internet. The GP is still seen as the main source of Primary care and the response implies that women are uncomfortable about not having access to information from this important source.

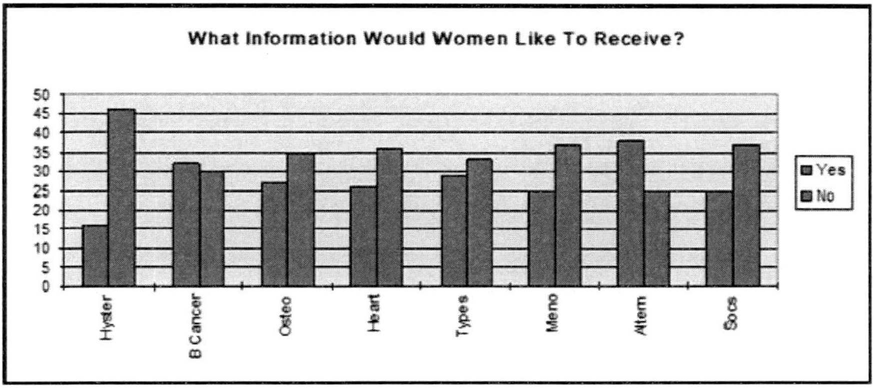

Figure 8

References

1. **Scriven. A.** Information Needs of Hysterectomy Patients. Nursing Standard, 9(7). 1994.

5. Discussion

The study has had several limitations. For the most part the respondents were a self selected group that were probably already aware of health management issues. This was particularly noticeable with the respondents that came from Women's Health and Here's Health. This may have presented a bias upon the results. In addition, the number of women that participated in the study was relatively small. It is therefore uncertain whether the results could be applied across the whole population and a separate study would be required to address this issue.

However, there are also positive points to the methods used to create the sample population. The women replying to the letter in Here's Health, those registered with Women's Health and the Personal respondents were drawn from all over the UK, therefore they represent an extended population, that will prevent bias on a regional basis and the researcher is not aware of their ethnic group. This has also enabled some comparative analysis with those respondents from the GP surgery lists. It has allowed discussion about whether a "good" GP makes a difference in offering the type of additional information a woman feels she needs, the service she receives and her later experience of taking HRT.

Initially, the study was hoping to look at women that were under the age of 50 when they had their hysterectomy, however, following discussions with a GP in Swadlincote, South Derbyshire it has to be noted that many surgeries do not have record systems that can easily identify women that have had a hysterectomy. The main method used was to pick out those that were not on recall lists for smear tests. The GP ventured that one of the reasons for this was the data protection act and a general reluctance to commit notes to computer[1]. Following this conversation the age restriction was dropped. Through later reading it also became apparent that women of any age, having a hysterectomy, could have health problems related to dropping testosterone and oestrogen levels. It became clear that the over 50's should not be ignored.

The data has been analysed in the following sections:

- General Health Information
- Hysterectomy Information
- Information about HRT
- Additional Sources of Information Used
- Information that is needed

There were also a number of additional analyses performed on the data, to consider the following questions:

1. Whether there was any difference in the information received or obtained from alternative sources by the different groups of women.
2. Whether there was any link between the reason for the surgery and type of hysterectomy performed.

3. Whether there was any relationship between women taking HRT and where the respondents came from, including the amount and type of information they were given and/or obtained themselves.

5.1 General Health Information Available In The Surgery

Health information is available in the surgeries of all the women that took part, as there were no women that did not answer this section of the questionnaire. However the data suggests that they did not necessarily have access to all the types listed.

5.2 Hysterectomy

The majority of surgery for hysterectomy is elective[2], meaning that the majority of woman have the surgery through choice rather than as a result of a life threatening illness. Out of 62 replies only four came from women that had had cancer.

Women that had surgery due to fibroids or endometriosis were more likely to have a 'total' hysterectomy than any other group (64% and 77% respectively); this does not include those that had surgery for cancers. Endometriosis can affect other organs in the abdomen and when it does a total hysterectomy can be justified. However fibroids are *usually* found within the uterus and it is interesting to note that many women have a total hysterectomy when the condition can be dealt with through either an endometrial oblation, D&C or myomectomy; procedures which act only on the lining of the womb. Those fibroids that occur on the outer wall of the uterus could be dealt with by partial hysterectomy. See tables in Appendix 12.

The surgery for cancer falls into two distinct groups. The true gynaecological cancers, uterine and ovarian, resulted in total hysterectomies, whereas cervical cancer resulted in a total hysterectomy in only 50% of cases. Perhaps this can be explained if cervical cancer is less likely to spread to other reproductive organs than the other two.

The results to the questions in this section are also interesting in that nine (14.5%) women reported having surgery for 'heavy bleeding'. This is interesting because this is a very subjective area, what is heavy for one woman can be light for another. If it was only bleeding that is the problem, why did 44% of the women that said they had had heavy bleeding report having a total hysterectomy? Bleeding is often a symptom of all other conditions that were listed in the questionnaire, apart from prolapse. It may not be too great an assumption that in these nine cases there was some other diagnosis as well, that either the woman was not aware of or did not understand.

The data also seems to suggest that although women had the opportunity to see their GP about the surgery, most of the women felt that the information they were given was not very helpful, that more often than not they did not feel that their questions were being answered and that they did not feel very well prepared for their surgery. However, there does appear to be a marked difference in attitude between the women that came from the two surgeries and all other groups.

However, data in Appendix 13 seems to indicate that women who completed questionnaires from the two surgeries in the study received more information, found it easier to understand and were able to discuss their surgery with their GP whenever they needed to more than women in any other group. They also appeared to be happier with the information they had received as they felt better prepared for the operation than their counterparts. Although the types of information that they received was similar to other groups fewer numbers reported that they had not received any information, in fact two woman reported that they had moved to one of the surgeries because of it's reputation for providing good care. The women also reported they received more information from their GP although there was no apparent difference in when they received the information. They were also less likely to feel the need to use additional sources of information.

5.3 Hormone Replacement Therapy

According to John Studd[3], currently only 12-16% of those women that can take HRT (for any reason, including hysterectomy) do so. Of the women that completed the questionnaire however, 62% said they were currently taking a form of HRT (two women said they were using a natural progesterone cream not available on prescription). This simple fact implies that women who have a hysterectomy are more aware of the benefits of the drug than other groups of women taking it to relieve menopause symptoms. However this compliance with treatment must be due to other factors as well, information being the most important.

None of the women who completed the questionnaire reported that they had been given information on alternatives to HRT. Perhaps this is not surprising as the NHS does not appear to support alternative therapies at present. This of course may explain why the information most requested later in the questionnaire was about the alternatives to HRT.

There seems to be some discrepancy about the information that women say they have had concerning HRT. Questions 7,13,14 and 15 all asked whether women had received information about HRT. The answers have been conflicting:

Question 7 - 40% of respondents said they *had* received information about HRT, this implies that 60% of women had not received information about HRT.

Question 13 - 45% of respondents said they had not received information about HRT from anyone, this implies that 55% *had* received information about HRT.

Question 14 - 35% said that they had not received information about HRT at any time, this implies that 65% *had* received information about HRT.

Question 15 - 38% said that they had not received any information about HRT, this implies that 62% *had* received information about HRT.

The difference between these answers can be seen in the next table.

Why this should be the case is not immediately obvious, perhaps the large difference recorded between question seven and all others could be because women thought the question was only considering information received *at the time* of their operation. In questions 14 and 15 women could have implied that they should consider *any* information received, from *whatever* source, whilst question 13 was only considering information received from healthcare professionals. These explanations may go some way to explaining the 25% difference reported between questions.

QUESTION No.	RECEIVED INFORMATION	NOT RECEIVED INFORMATION
7	**40%**	**60%**
13	**55%**	**45%**
14	**65%**	**35%**
15	**62%**	**38%**

TABLE 1

Another surprising feature of the responses was that four women (6.4%) reported the use of audio tapes to present information about HRT (Question 19). This is surprising as question four showed a response rate of 1.6% (one woman) to the use of audio tapes to present health information. The point that this appears to make is that either women are not aware of information or what constitutes 'information' within a general practice setting, or that they had received tapes from additional sources rather than medical services.

Eight women (12.9%) reported receiving information about HRT in the form of drug company leaflets, yet in question 19 this figure soars to 25 (40%) of women. Why this should be different can only be explained if we assume that the additional numbers of women read the leaflets that came with their prescription and did not consider these to be 'information'. There are a number of leaflets about related issues, such as osteoporosis, heart disease, menopause etc.. that are also sponsored by the drug companies: these may be the 'information' that women assumed the question was referring to.

Data in Appendix 14 indicates that women that are taking tablets or are using patches received more information about more subjects than any other group, although those taking tablets were much less likely than any other group not to receive information about their HRT from their GP or consultant. The same criteria can be applied to those using additional sources of information; those women taking tablets recorded a significantly higher use of almost all additional sources of information than any other users of HRT. This seems to suggest that women will seek out information if they are not given it, in order to confirm their compliance with treatment.

There appears to be no difference in the source amongst women who said they were taking HRT. All five groups seemed to be just as likely to take HRT as any other. Women were more likely to take HRT in all age groups apart from the 20-30 years of age category. However, as there was only one respondent in the 20-30 years of age category, this cannot be a fair comparison. There must be some other unifying factor that results in women taking HRT.

Data in Appendix 17 seems to indicate that being given information from a healthcare professional makes women more likely to take HRT than those that had not been given information in this way and in all cases receiving *any* information about issues related to HRT, even breast cancer, resulted in larger numbers using HRT than those that had not had any at all.

Interestingly though, receiving information about the menopause did not greatly influence the number of women taking the drug as only 62% recorded that they had received information about this subject. Perhaps we can assume then that women are taking HRT following hysterectomy not simply to alleviate menopausal symptoms but to protect their general long term health (however, it may just be because they have been told to). In all cases, apart from two, the women using additional information sources were more likely to take HRT than not. From this data we can go on to make the assumption that having access to numerous sources of information increases women's feelings of ease with HRT and together with the knowledge of the risks helps them to make informed choices. Those women that had not had any information about HRT or used fewer sources of additional information did not record the same usage.

5.4 Additional Sources Of Information Used By Women

As 84% of women did report using additional sources of information and that they have tended to use more than one source would indicate that they feel their need for quality information has not been met by the healthcare system. However, it is interesting to note that those women from the two surgeries who completed questionnaires used fewer alternative sources than any other group, perhaps because they felt more confident with the information they had received at the outset. We may also make the assumption that the fact that so many women use non-professional forms of information to supplement what they have been given by the medical profession could explain why there is so much myth surrounding hysterectomy and HRT, although this doesn't seem to impact greatly on the use of HRT.

5.5 Information Required By Women

The data seems to indicate that whilst only 19% of women recorded receiving most of their information about HRT from their GP, 58% feel that this is the most appropriate place to get it. The fact that those women drawn from Stamford and Wokingham used fewer additional sources of information also serves to support this assumption. Figure eight (chapter on results) shows that the subjects women want most information about are alternatives to HRT and breast cancer. So whilst information results in a greater use of HRT, this suggests that there is still the desire to use something more natural. These replies of course support the answers that were received in question 12, where no women reported receiving information on alternatives to HRT and only 12 (19%) said that they had received anything about Breast Cancer.

5.6 Changes To The Questionnaire

There were a number of changes to the questionnaire that may have had an affect on the results if the questions had been phrased differently. For instance it may have been possible to analyse the effect of age on information received if the researcher was sure about the age of the respondent when they had their surgery.

It may have been possible to consider the positive effect that information about hysterectomy had on patient experience, if it had been known how the information was presented to the patient. As the study in Bath has shown, information in any form did have a positive effect on the experience of hysterectomy patients. Throughout the questionnaire there has been no mention of verbal information, yet this may have been the largest type of information given.

In question 12, rather than offering women two options to say that no information was received from the GP or the Consultant and where the replies produced ambiguous results, it may have been better to phrase the reply as 'I did not receive any information about HRT from my GP or my Consultant. This would have produced an easier analysis. As it stands the information gleaned from this section is valid only if the assumption is made that patients did not receive any information from either source.

Throughout the questionnaire there should have been clearer indications that the information being considered was only that received from healthcare professionals unless otherwise specifically stated. Although most women seem to have made this assumption it is a factor that must be taken into account particularly when considering the answers to questions asking about information received on HRT.

The original questions of whether a 'good' GP makes a difference and whether the types and amounts of information make a difference in patients compliance with HRT treatment have produced some interesting answers then. The data suggests that where a patient considers a GP to be providing the information she requires, she records better care in general and will use fewer sources of additional information compared to other groups, although she will still use additional sources of information. However, when considering whether receipt of information plays a role in patient compliance with HRT, it appears that women receiving *any* amount of information from a professional will be more inclined to take the drug, than those that hadn't and if they feel they have not had enough they will seek out other information to support their decision.

There is still a question mark over whether the information received about the type of surgery necessary makes a difference to whether women will go on to have surgery or if they will question the type of operation to be performed. This analysis was not performed, as more detailed data would be necessary to adequately consider it.

References

1. Interview with Dr J. Kirk, Darklands Road Surgery, Swadlincote. 15/03/97.
2. **Gann, R.** *The Health Information Handbook*; Gower Publishing Company Limited, Aldershot. 1986.
3. **Khastgir, G. and J. Studd.** *Hysterectomy and HRT*. in press.

6. Building An Information Resource

There were two deliverables required by the study. The first was a quality web resource and the second was to produce a sample booklet that could be given to women having a hysterectomy. Both of these were to contain information important to women in the areas indicated by the results of the questionnaires.

6.1 Publishing On The Internet

Publishing health information on the Internet, is the most simple way to self publish information. However, there are a number of issues that should be considered where possible:

- anyone can publish information on the Internet and on occasions the patient can be more expert than the experts simply because they are specialising in only one limited area. However, on the whole, the information has not necessarily been accepted by the medical profession and at best should be taken at face value only. Well referenced sites allow a user to check the credibility of the author and bibliographies allow them to read further.
- there is little control over how the site will look on another computer or browser.
- there is a lack of true audience measurement tools that are used in other broadcast media.
- it is difficult for users to locate information that is useful.

- authors should consider whether or not to ask for payment for information provided on the site.
- the number of people using the Internet is small at present, but it is growing all the time.
- the Internet allows the user to interact with the author through the use of email and forms.
- all users will navigate through a site differently and easy navigation tools are essential.
- users expect authors to keep the sites up to date and will look for new material on a regular basis.

6.1.1 The Internet, Good And Bad

The Internet is a medium totally unlike any other used before. It isn't linear, in the same way as a book, radio broadcast or television programme is. Magazines and newspapers are more interactive as their readers can access the information they require in a random fashion. But the amount of information is limited to what can be put on to the number of pages available.

Within a traditional broadcast medium, the content is prepared and is passed on to the user/consumer via the most appropriate method, this may be magazine or book or television. It is a one way, one to many process in which the user plays a very passive role. The Interent on the other hand is highly interactive and allows users to access information from a number of sources. It allows people the opportunity to make educated and informed choices about everything, including their health. Traditional publishing can be very solitary, it may refer to other publications but it cannot build on them. A book, for instance, has to be taken at face value unless there are others within easy reach to add to the content or confirm it. An Internet site designer on the other hand does not have to prepare the content of the site exhaustively in the same way that a writer would have to. Hypertext documents can link to other documents to illustrate a point or provide more in-depth information. On the Internet it is not necessary to re-invent the wheel by covering information that is well represented elsewhere. It can be said that as the number of people contributing to the wealth of knowledge that is the Internet grows, the value of the knowledge grows and deepens. The result of this process is the Information community that many talk of already, it consists of many thousands of people across the world sharing varying levels of commitment and knowledge.

According to Denis Anthony, a National Opinion Poll that was recently conducted showed that 2.35 million people had used the Internet in the previous 12 months in the UK (about 5% of the population)[1]. Chris Dowd has also said

> *"although no-one would confidently predict what the Internet will look like or be capable of ten years from now, it is likely to have matured into a technology that one takes for granted much in the way that they telephone and television are accepted today"*[2].

The Internet provides an information democracy. As long as the information is available, anyone with access to the web can access it. In traditional business terms the phrase 'position, position, position' does not hold true with the Internet as all web pages are equally accessible technically, wherever they are world-wide. Once a document has been placed on the Internet, it costs nothing to distribute it. Every time the site is accessed a copy of the document is transmitted via the Internet.

There are two ways to present information on the Internet. Sites can be linear, in that the information is presented in a very strict sequence, this appropriate for those subjects that have an element of teaching in them. The navigation is structured in such a way that it builds on knowledge already gained and understood. The site can also be semantic so that information can be accessed from many different points of view according to an individual users needs. They don't need to know about A before they read about C, if it is C that interests them. This means that the author of the work needs to surrender control over access, and navigation to the users. Of course sites can be combinations of linear and semantic and many sites are presented in this way.

6.1.2 Publicising The Site

Perhaps the biggest disability to publishing on the Internet, is the difficulty finding relevant information simply by 'surfing'. Just about anybody can put up a page or a complete site for relatively little cost. In 1996 it was estimated that there were about five million documents already available[3]. Finding a resource that is useful could be like finding a needle in the proverbial haystack. Site designers therefore rely on advertising their sites and there are two main marketing methods used (both are similar to those used in other media):

- Direct publicity - to newsgroups or mailing lists, or people that you know
- Indirect publicity - submitting to search engines, what's new pages

In some ways, the considerations could be compared to those of booksellers; they do not have the room to stock all of the books available for every subject and the facility to order books relies on the systems that they use to identify what is (available). The author of a book also has to understand these problems as well. They need to target an audience (say a business community) and then market the book in the most appropriate way, this may be through journals or professional associations. The book may then be sold via the association or it may be available through a specialist book seller. Publishing on the Internet has to be approached in very similar ways.

Identify the target audience and then advertise the site to them. This inevitably means registering with some or all of the popular search engines; using subject gateways for specialist information and using appropriate mailing lists or discussion groups. The site address can also be registered with a "what's' new" site or it could also be announced on the ISP (Internet Service Provider) or on the newsgroup, comp.infosystems.www.announce.

Direct mail, can be irritating when it comes through the letter box and this is no less the case for email. Many thousands of email boxes are filled each day with postings that will never be opened. Maybe this is because of the much quoted "information overload". More often it may be because the title is obscure and doesn't attract the attention of those that would be interested if only they knew it.

Another method of indirect advertising is to contact other sites that are also interested in the subject area. This is also a useful way of gaining support. They may offer reciprocal links between the sites, in which case both will benefit from the different marketing strategies being used by each.

6.1.3 Measuring The Audience

Once the site is on the web it is useful to know who is accessing it and why. There are currently very few audience measurement tools available for the Internet. Perhaps the most widely used tool is the web counter. This records the number of *hits* a page receives (that is the number of times a pages is accessed by someone). The difficulty with it is that it does not discriminate between those people that access the site deliberately and those that come across it by accident in their travels. It is also important to remember that the web counter counts the number of files that have been accessed on a page, where there are several images this will inflate the number of hits recorded for *each* person accessing the page. As it only records the page on which it is placed, the author has no way of knowing whether people have gone on elsewhere within the site.

Another way of gaining useful market information about who is accessing the site is to build in some form of audience response tool. This enables the user to let the author know what they think of the site. They can take the form of structured questionnaires (forms) or email messages for comments. Questionnaires can be sent to the author in two ways, they can be emailed direct to the author in which case they will need to take out the coding sent with it or they can be sent though a CGI (Common Gateway Interface) this presents the information as a report, it also requires programming skills.

6.1.4 Site Design

There is considerable current debate about how a site should be designed. Some say that it should cater for the lowest common denominator and allow those without access to graphical browsers and who have slow modems to access the content. Others say that the design is the most important element and as most people have graphical browsers, people will only look at sites that look good. The final design of a site may depend, at the end of the day, on who the target audience is.

Designing for the lowest common denominator: a slow machine with a slow dial up modem access and no graphical browser will involve limited use of graphics, especially large ones as the bandwidth needed to transmit images is large. If graphics are used adding an "alt image" tag to them allows the user to understand what the image is even if they cannot see it, particularly important if used as a hyperlink. Limiting the number of colours used on the site, will also decrease the download time.

Some of the newer HTML tags are not supported by all browsers: these include tables, frames and some advanced formatting tags. However Netscape, Mosaic and Internet Explorer are the most popular browsers and these support the most common higher level HTML tags[4].

6.2 Producing The Hysterectomy Support Pages

People working in healthcare are increasingly under pressure to be aware of all of the latest advances in medicine, however with pressure on their time also increasing this becomes very difficult. The Internet can provide access to "timely, accurate and validated"[5], information at the touch of a button, any time of the day and at the moment of need. This applies not only to the medical profession, but is equally true for consumers of healthcare. The site has been created to meet this need, to provide information professionals may use but in a readable format that consumers can also appreciate.

The site has been designed to allow maintenance following the completion of the degree. It consists of a single level of information, all pages accessible through links embedded within a table that appears at the top of each page. The site has been designed as a semantic net passing control over navigation to the consumer. Users can take as much or as little information as they need from the site and can see at a glance where they may want to go. The structure of the database is shown in Appendix three. There are four main areas to the information:

Hysterectomy, what it is and why it might become necessary and the effects it may have on women.

The menopause, what it is, the symptoms and some of the other implications of the menopause with a particular emphasis on those women that have had an early menopause due to surgery.

Hormone Replacement Therapy, why it is necessary, what it is, the types available and the alternative ways of dealing with the menopause

Support networks, further information and links to other useful site. This section also includes a glossary to explain some of the terminology.

Following the results of the study, the latter three were the areas that women said that they would like to have more information on. Although some women said that they would like more information about hysterectomy, it was not as high a priority, probably due to the fact that they had already had the operation. However, the American Site - Sans Uteri[6], shows that women do want access to information about hysterectomy before they have the operation, so that they can understand all of the implications. The discussion list held on Sans-Uteri indicates that women feel a need for the information so that they can make an informed choice.

There is minimal use of graphics which will decrease the download time. The Hysterectomy Support Pages use four graphics within the information pages, these are the green ball image used to display unordered lists, the green bar image that separates and divides the text elements within in each page, an up-arrow at the bottom of the page that takes the user back to the top of the page without having to scroll through and a back arrow at the top of each page that allows the user to return to the home page. They are all under 1K in size and those that are used have 'alt image' tags.

Several tables are used within the site to make navigation easier and to define information. There is also an evaluation form that is accessible from the home page. The site is designed in this way to make it easy for the user to identify information rather than be distracted by material not as relevant to them.

Navigation is via the table that appears at the top of each page of information apart from the home page. The pages within the third level of information are accessed from the Menopause and Hormone Replacement Therapy sections of the site and each have a secondary table on them that enables navigation within that particular section of the site. Some other HTML 3 tags have been used within the documents, however these are used to enhance text areas and should be ignored by browsers not using them. The same applies to the colour background, on those computers/browsers that do not have the capability to display it the background will appear white.

All pages are at the same level on the server and no hierarchy has been used in the creation of pages, this was a decision made as a result of the long file names that would result because of the server it is placed on. Should the site be moved to another server the hierarchy that applies to the information would be applied to the file management. The site has been mounted on the UK Online server, a commercial Internet provider which offers unlimited web space to it's members. The address of the site is:

http://web.ukonline.co.uk/linda.newall/index.htm

The site has been rated with RASC (parental control system)[7], so that the rating system for parental control can be applied. Although it is a site designed to provide medical information to the consumer, there is some content that parents may not wish their children to see.

To aid the indexing of the site on search engines Dublin Core metadata has been included in the headings this defines the key words used. Not all automatic search engines use metadata tags and the method used for indexing the pages with these has been applying appropriate titles for each pages specifically identifying the content.

The site has been marketed extensively and the URL has been submitted to the following (although it has not necessarily been accepted by all):

Search Engines

- Yahoo - http://www.yahoo.com (accepted)
- Altavista - http://www.altavista.com (accepted)
- Lycos - http://www.lycos.com (accepted)
- Excite - http://www.excite.com

What's new sites:

- Starting Point - http://www.stpt.com (accepted)
- AAA World Wide Announce Archive - http://www.aaa.com.au/ (accepted)
- WebPromote - http://www.WebPromote.com/de (accepted)

Subject Gateways:

- OMNI - http://omni.ac.uk

Sites:

- Sans Uteri - http://www.2cowherd.net/findings/ (accepted)
- Marie Stopes Clinics - http://www.mariestopes.org.uk
- National Osteoporosis Society - http://www.nos.org.uk/

Information about the site has also been sent to Women's Health, The Amarant Trust and Here's Health.

6.3 Producing A Consumer Health Information Booklet

Perhaps the most popular of the consumer health information available is the consumer health information leaflet or booklet. These can be found at surgeries, dentists waiting rooms, pharmacies and hospital departments. They are the most usual way for support organisations to produce literature about a particular disease or condition. However, many of them are also produced by the drug companies that make HRT and these are often distributed free of charge to GP's for use by their patients.

They are also cheap, by comparison to books, do not need to be marketed in the same way that books and magazines do and can be self published by a health authority, NHS department, GP, Hospital or organisation knowing that only those interested in the subject or within a particular catchement area will require one.

The format of a booklet is, of essence, linear. The patient starts at the beginning and works their way through to the end. It is possible that patients may use the booklet in the same way that they use a web site, they dip in and only take out the information that they require. However this is difficult without extensive contents pages and indexes and requires a knowledge of the subject to begin with. There is also a limit to the amount of information included and it is not interactive.

There are several ways to produce booklets and leaflets. They can be self published and sent to people requesting them for a small fee however, this limits the market available. They could be sponsored by an organisation, but this takes time and they would still not be widely available unless requested. They could be published and put on general release although it may be difficult to have a manuscript accepted without having medical qualifications and again it may not be carried by all book sellers and/or libraries.

Perhaps the biggest drawback of publishing in this way is that the information may be limited to a particular country, region or even surgery. The information contained in the booklet also suffers from lack of currency. It may be out of date quickly and it is thus costly to keep updating the booklet to take account of these changes in a way that the Web site is not.

6.4 Producing The Hysterectomy Information Booklet

The booklet takes the information produced for the web site and presents the most important elements in a straight forward linear style. The main areas of interest are:

- Information about hysterectomy
- The menopause
- Hormone Replacement Therapy
- Support groups and further reading

There is information about the web site, indicating that it is updated on a regular basis and contains links to other sites that may be of interest.

The booklet is being marketed in several ways. Those women that took part in the study will receive details of the results of the survey and can request a copy of the booklet. The GP's that took part will receive a copy of the results and the booklet. The manuscript will be sent to the various support organisations to see if they will take it up and or publicise it in their newsletters. It will also be sent to some appropriate publishing companies.

References

1. **Anthony, D**. *Health on the Internet*. Blackwell Science Limited, London. 1996. p.xi.
2. **Dowd, C**. in *Health on the Internet*. Blackwell Science Limited, London. 1996. p.xii.
3. **Pfaffenberger, B**. Publish It On The Web; Academic Press Limited, London1996; p54.
4. Ibid; p273
5. **Dowd, C**. ref. 2. p.xi
6. **Sans Uteri**. (URL: http://www.2cowherd.net/findings/), 18/08/97.
7. RASC (Recreational software advisory council on the Internet), (URL: http://www.rasc.org/), 18/08/97.

7. Conclusions

There appears to be no doubt that women feel they are not being given enough information about either their hysterectomy or Hormone Replacement Therapy. Even where women said that they had received information about particular subjects, they were a minority in almost every case and there appears to be no standard practice followed within the NHS.

The majority of the women that completed questionnaires also made additional comments about their treatment. Whilst there were a minority (mainly from the surgeries) that said they were happy with the treatment and information they had received, the vast majority were not happy and two women said that they had changed to one of the two surgeries to receive better care. One respondent, a librarian, commented

"I was delighted to see that some research is being carried out on this important topic. It is still very neglected, and women are not being informed and suffer as a consequence"

She also went on to say *"I am now much more assertive in asking questions and demanding information since the first op. Sadly, my second op. demonstrated that hospitals are not offering information on these topics and fellow patients were very uniformed."* This sentiment seems to be true across the majority of respondents.

The types of information that a patient receives from the medical professionals when they have a hysterectomy appears to depend to a great extent on the patient, the GP and the type of relationship that exists between the two. A patient that asks questions will, naturally, receive more information than a patient who accepts without question. As one patient said, whilst she did get information it was only *after* asking questions or presenting her own facts. There is considerable evidence that GP's and consultants are more than happy to answer any questions that a patient may have, but it is complicated further if a woman does not know what to ask about in the first place. There may also be a tendency on the part of the consultant to assume that if a woman doesn't ask questions that she has already been given all the information she needs by the GP, and vice versa. The patient then gets caught in the middle with no way out.

Whilst the importance of the relationship between GP and patient may appear to be stating the obvious, the patients charter also requires that any treatment is fully described and explained to a patient. There is also the new Hippocratic Oath to be taken into consideration. It is currently under discussion with the World Health Organisation and states that doctors should ensure that patients receive information that helps them to make decisions about their health, from a point of knowledge.

However, it has been suggested that women don't ask questions because they don't want to take an active part in their health management. Angela Scriven said *"the avoidance of information may be a coping strategy"*. However, if a woman is not given time to think about what has been said they may not know what to say or how to ask for help. Even if women say that don't want to be given information at the outset, this is no reason for not giving it to them. Information is power, it gives a patient the power to make a choice for themselves, if they avoid the information as a coping strategy by ripping up the booklet, they have still made a choice to do that.

There is also an indisputable link between a person's perception of what is "care" and the amount of information received. Those women that had said they were happy with their care reported better access to information from their GP and they also used fewer additional sources. Perhaps patients feel that "care" in the NHS is the feeling that there is someone that thinks of their welfare enough to give them information. It is not necessarily the information that they receive that is important but rather the act of giving. This correlation between the perception of care and information can be better understood when you consider the fact that those women that had received some information (any amount, in any format) actually recovered more quickly and had fewer post-operative problems than those women that had not been given any information at all. This may simply be because a woman does not have any false expectations/understandings about her surgery and long term health there after.

If there is a link between health after surgery and information, it may be agreed that it is in the best interests of the NHS to improve the standards of patient health information. Costs could be reduced considerably; prevention being better and cheaper than cure. A typical scenario may be the woman who, twelve months after surgery, goes to her doctor saying she can't sleep and is often weepy, it is summer so she doesn't mention the sweating at night. The GP, pressured as they are, doesn't connect these symptoms with her hysterectomy and suggests counselling or a course of anti-depressants (far fetched? - it does happen frequently) the costs to the NHS goes up. If a woman were aware of all the likely outcomes of her surgery at the outset, she would be better placed to recognise the symptoms and take appropriate action.

The path that leads to hysterectomy may well look like this:

Initial appointment with GP - Explanation of symptoms

⇩

Referred to gynaecologist

⇩

Tests - usually in-patient

⇩

Results of Tests and Diagnosis - This is probably the first time a woman will be told she needs a hysterectomy

⇩

Surgery

⇩

Six week check-up- Usually as an out-patient.

The majority of women said that their preferred source of information was their GP. One woman commented *"the GP should always have information but a library would be an ideal place to get information without bothering your GP"*. However, identifying the correct point of delivery in the above process is crucial. As it is the consultant that will, more often than not, tell a woman she needs a hysterectomy maybe this should be the correct point of delivery rather than the GP. A woman's GP can be used to provide additional information, support or help after she has read the literature already provided.

The surgery is, in the main, supposed to be elective. However once diagnosed and on the 'conveyor belt' towards surgery it is very difficult for a woman to get off and without adequate information about choices that is timely, appropriate and valid at the correct time she may never be able to. The process demonstrated above becomes a process of submission not election, if there is no information given.

As I said earlier, the relationship a patient has with her GP is particularly important and those GP's that took part in the study came highly recommended by their patients. One woman commented *"My GP is most helpful on any matter discussed with him"*. It would be very easy to assume that the lack of response from other GP's indicates they may feel they are failing their patients. However, GP's are under increasing pressure of time. They have to hold knowledge of many thousands of different conditions and treatments. They have increasingly larger lists and management responsibilities take them away from what they joined the profession to do.

The study suggests that the majority of information women receive comes from mass media sources. These, in addition to being possible providers of misinformation, may also increase stress and anxiety about taking HRT. Disinformation can only be refuted when 'good' information has already been received.

To remedy this problem perhaps the use of information professionals attached to surgeries that can provide information about health topics to both GP's and patients alike could be advocated. Those surgeries that have access to a web browser could put sites found on the Internet on a computer that patients can have access to, together with leaflets, books, videos and tapes for patients to borrow.

The Hysterectomy Support Pages have already generated interest from women, one said that she *"found the material very informative and answered some of the questions my doctor did not"*. The web site will be maintained and further developed following the completion of the study. That use of the Internet is growing cannot be disputed, a recent interview on Radio 2's Debbie Thrower programme with the Marketing Director of Yahoo, Europe, indicated that women that are in their 30's - 40's are a powerful emergent market. Just the sector that wants good, quality information about their health. There are probably some that might like to suggest that the Internet is a passing fad, but I would like to suggest that is like radio, difficult to do without 'Evidence' is already provided by the numerous other media that have embraced it wholeheartedly, including newspapers, radio and television programmes, manufacturers also give their URL in advertisements and the ubiquitous 'home page' is becoming the latest designer tool, rather like the mobile 'phone two or three years ago.

At the outset of this study, I had assumed that any findings about a patients need for information could be applied across the range of conditions found in health care. However, at this point I have to say I do not think it can. Women feel very strongly about hysterectomy, the comments I have had from women taking part confirm this. Perhaps the depth of feeling is associated with the fact that this surgery cuts to the very heart of what being a woman is all about.

In a rapidly changing world, where market forces rule and loss of humanity is endemic, it may be necessary to refocus on the Person. The journey of a thousand miles begins with the first step. I would like this study to be that first step to regaining our emphasis on our humanity.

Bibliography

Aloia, J.F. *Osteoporosis: A guide to prevention and treatment*. Leisure Press, Illinois, USA. 1989.

Amarant Trust. *Alternatives to HRT at the menopause*. Amarant Trust, London. 1997.

Amarant Trust. *Information Leaflet*. London. 1997.

Amarant Trust. *HRT and me*. Amarant Trust, London. 1997.

Amarant Trust. *HRT and the menopause: treatment updates*. Amarant Trust, London. 1997.

Anthony, D. Health on the Internet. Blackwell Science Limited, London. 1996.

Audit Commission. *What seems to be the matter? the communication between hospitals and patients*. H.M.S.O. 1993.

Bailey, J. *HRT and Cardio-Protection: Unravelling the Tangled Web.* European Menopause Journal Symposium Report, 4(1). 1996. (URL: http://www.medscape.com/PMSI/EMJ/1..01.05.bailey/em0401.05.bailey.html), 14/05/97.

Bandolier. *HRT and Breast Cancer*. (URL: http://www.jr2.ox.ac.uk/Bandolier/band24/b24-2.html) 7 Jan. 1997; 21 Jan 1997.

Bewley, S and T.H. Bewley. *Drug dependence with oestrogen replacement therapy*. The Lancet, 339. 1 Feb. 1992.

Bergstrom, R, and M. Falkeboom. *Hormone Replacement Therapy and the risk of strokes: Follow up of a population based cohort in Sweden.* Archives of Internal Medicine, 153(10). 1993.

BMA Press Releases. *BMA updates Hippocratic Oath.*

(URL: http://www.bma.org/pressrel/archive/970327b.htm), 28/03/97, 20/08/97.

Bloomsbury Publishing Ltd. *Medicines: The comprehensive guide.* Paragon Book Service Limited, London. 1995.

Boulton, A. *Hormone Therapy may protect against Alzheimer's Disease.* British Medical Journal, 313. 1996.

Burger, C.W and I.Koomen, N.A.J.B. Peters, F.E. Van Leeuwen, P. Kenemans. *Postmenopausal Hormone Replacement Therapy and Cancer of the Female Genital Tract and the Breast*. European Menopause Journal, 4(1). 1997. (URL: http://www.medscape.co.uk/PMSI/EMJ/1...01.04.burger/em0401.04.burger.html), 05/07/97.

Cabot, Dr S. *The Menopause Handbook*. Boxtree limited, London. 1996.

Carron, L. *Hormone replacement does not promote recurrence in breast-cancer patients*. Medical Tribune, Obstetrician and Gynaecologist Edition, 4(4). 1997. (URL: http://www.medscape.com/jobson/Med...04.no04/Hormone%BreastCancer.htm), 1604/97.

Cochrane, A. *Hormones Special Report.* Here's Health, London. 10/92.
Conjugated Estrogens. (URL: http://www.rxlist.com), 1997, 22/04/97.

Denke, M.A. Hormone Replacement Therapy: benefit and safety issues. Current Opinion in Lipidology, 7. 1996. (URL: http://biomednet.com/), 1803/97.

Deny, M. *Informed consent, emotional responses of patients.* Postgraduate Medicine, 60(5). 1975.

Department of Health. *The Patients Charter*. H.M.S.O. 1991.

Dover, C. *Ward Lock Family Health Guide - Osteoporosis*. Ward Lock, London. 1994.

Doyle, C. *Why all the hysteria?* The Daily Telegraph, London. 25/02/97.

Edwards, M. *Information and education for patients and health care professionals*. European Menopause Journal, 3(2). 1997. (URL: http://www.medscape.com/PMSI/EMJ/1....07.edwards/em0302.07.edwards.html), 18/02/97.

Effectiveness Review Bulletin. *Osteoporosis*; Bandolier; (URL: http://www.jr2.ox.ac.uk:80/Bandolier/band3/b3-4.html); 18/02/97.

Estradiol (transdermal). (URL: http://www.rxlist.com/), 1997, 22/04/97.

European Menopause Journal. *HRT and venous thromboembolism*. European Menopause Journal, 3(4). 1996. (URL: http://www.medscape.com/PMSI/EMJ/), 18/02/97.

Ferriman, A. *Getting hooked on HRT.* The Independent, Section two, London. 02/07/96.

Ferriman, A. *Osteoporosis*. HealthFront, Daily Telegraph Magazine. London. 09/03/97.

Finch, P. *How to publish yourself*. WH Allen and Co, London. 1987.

Francis, A. *The new HRT (herbs that is, not hormones).* Daily Mail, London. 31/10/95.

Gann, R. *The Health Information Handbook*. Gower Publishing Company Limited, Aldershot. 1986.

Glenville, Dr. M. *Natural alternatives to HRT*. Kyle Cathie Limited, London. 1997.

Glew, J. *The Menopause*. Here's Health. 07/97.

Greenfield, T.(ed). *Research methods: guidance for postgraduates*. Arnold, Hodder Headline Group, London. 1996.

Hampson, A. *Brittle Words: The impact of health information on patients compliance with treatment*. M.A. Dissertation, Department of Information and Library Studies, Loughborough University of Technology. 1995.

Harding, C. and W.F. Knox, E.B. Faragher, A. Baildam, N.J. Bundred. *Hormone replacement therapy and tumour grade in breast cancer: Prospective study in screening unit.* British Medical Journal, 312(7047). 1996.

Henderson, B. *An epidemiological evaluation of the risks and benefits of Hormone Replacement Therapy*. Proceedings of the inaugural scientific meeting of the American Menopause Society; Brisbane, Australia. Australian Menopause Society. 09/97.

Helstrom, L. and P.O. Lundberg, D. Sorbom, T. Backstrom. *Sexuality after hysterectomy; a factor analysis of women's sexual lives before and after hysterectomy.* Obstetric Gynaecology 81. 1993.

Hicks, C. *Funny bones who's laughing?* The Independent. London. 06/02/96.

Holford, P. *Be healthy, be happy without HRT.* Here's Health, London. 03/95.

Hope, J. *The perils of replacing HRT with ' natural supplements'.* Daily Mail, London. 20/02/96.

Jobson Healthcare Group. *Do long-term hormone replacement therapy benefits outweigh the risks?* Medical Tribune: Family Physician Edition, 38(9). 1997. (URL: http://www.medscape.com/jobson/Med...09/DoLongTermHRTBenefit /Risk.html), 1405/97.

Jones, B.N and J.R. Absher. *Estrogen and Alzheimers Disease: What is the connection?* Medscape Mental Health, 2(7). 1997. (URL: http://www.medscape.com/Medscape/M...n07/mh3273.jones.html), 08/06/97.

Lilford, R.J. *Hysterectomy: will it pay the bills in 2007?* British Medical Journal, 314(7075). 1997. (URL: http://biomednet.com/cgi-bin/fulltext/deliver.pl?uid=bm1306) 18/02/97.

Kaplin, Dr F.S. *Osteoporosis, Pathophysiology and Prevention.* Clinical Symposia 39(1). 1987.

Khastgir, G. and J. Studd. *Hysterectomy and HRT.* in press.

Knight, S.T. *Invitation to Truth, health knowledge and information.* M.Phil Dissertation. Department of Information and Library Studies, Loughborough University of Technology. 1990.

Laurence, L. *What every woman must know before menopause.* Readers Digest. London. 02/97.

Lavery, S. *Aromatherapy saved my from hysterectomy.* Here's Health, London. 12/94.

Ley, P. and P.W. Bradshaw, D. Eaves, C.M. Walker. *A method for increasing patients recall of information presented by Doctors.* Psychological Medicine, 3. 1989.

Ley P. *Improving clinical communication.* In: Oborne, D., Gruneberg, M.M., Euer, J.R. Research in Psychology and Medicine. Academic Press, London. 1997.

McLean, S. *A patients right to know.* Dartmouth Publishing Company, Aldershot. 1989.

Mann, D. *Breast cancer may be linked to bone density.* Medical Tribune: Family Physician Edition, 37(21). 1996. (URL: http://www.medscape.com/jobson/Med...7.n21/BreastCABoneDensity Risk.html), 20/02/97.

Mann, D. *HRT prolongs most women's lives - study concludes.* Medical Tribune: Family Physician Edition, 38(9). 1997.

(URL: http://www.medscape.com/), 14/05/97.

Marton, I. *Hormonal replacement therapy and cancer*. European Menopause Journal, 3(1). 1996. (URL: http://www.medscape.com/), 17/04/97.

M.D. Anderson Cancer Center. *Fallopian Tube Cancer*. (URL: http://143.111.212.41/dzsite_tube.html), 1996, 20/08/97.

Medical Research Council's General Practice Research Framework. *Randomised comparison of oestrogen versus oestrogen plus progestogen hormone replacement therapy in women with hysterectomy*. British Medical Journal, 312(4738). 1997.

Microsoft ® Encarta. Microsoft Corporation. 1994.

Modeca, P. *Raised bone mass linked to risk of breast cancer*. Medical Tribune: Internist and Cardiologist Edition, 38(7). 1997. (URL: http://www.medscape.com/jobson/Med...07/RaisedBoneMassBreastCancer.html), 16/04/97.

Moerman C.J. and J.C.M. Witteman, H.J.A. Collette, C. Gevers Leuven, C. Kluft, P. Kenemans, K. Meeter. *Hormone Replacement Therapy: A useful tool in the prevention of coronary artery disease in postmenopausal women*. European Menopause Journal, 3(2); 1996. (URL: http://www.medscape.com/PMSI/EMJ/1....04.moerman/em0302.04.moerman.html), 14/03/97.

Morris D. *Hormone replacement therapy and coronary heart disease*. Current Opinion in Obstetrics and Gynaecology, 8. 1996. (URL: http://biomednet.com/cgi-bin/fulltext/deliver.pl?uid=ob8306), 14/03/97.

National Osteoporosis Society.*You've had a hysterectomy*. National Osteoporosis Society, London. 1996.

Newall, L. *Informed Choice*. Here's Health. London. 07/97.

Newall, L. *Research Study*. EMIS User Group Magazine. Nottingham. 06/97.

Nicol, R. *Hormone Replacement Therapy*. Vermillion, Ebury Press, London. 1993.

Okon, M.A. and S. Lee, T.C. Li. *A Study to Examine Women's Knowledge, Perception and Acceptability of Hormone Replacement Therapy*. European Menopause Journal, 3(2). 1996. (URL: http://www.medscape.com/PMSI/EMJ/1...em0302.02.okon/em0302.02.okon.html), 15/04/97.

Pfaffenberger, B. *Publish It On The Web.* Academic Press Limited, London. 1996.

Planned Parenthood of America. *Hormone Replacement Therapy and alternative therapies.* Medical Strategies Inc. 1996. (URL: http://healthtouch.com/), 20/12/96.

Planned Parenthood of America. *Menopause*: Another change of life. Medical Strategies Inc. 1996. (URL: http://healthtouch.com/), 20/12/96.

Rees, A.M.(ed). *Osteoporosis*; Consumer Health USA. Oryx Press, Phoenix. 1995. (URL: http://www.medscape.com/Oryx/CHUSA/c21/a12.html), 20/02/97.

Reuben, Dr. D. *Good news about HRT.* Readers Digest. 08/97.

Rich-Edwards, J.W. and C. Hennekens. *Postmenopausal hormones and coronary heart disease.* Review Article, Current Opinion in Cardiology, 11. 1996.

Scriven. A. *Information Needs of Hysterectomy Patients.* Nursing Standard, 9(7). 1994.

Sethi, K. and J.Pitkin. *HRT Uptake and Compliance.* European Menopause Journal, 2(4). 1995. (URL: http://www.medscape.com/PMSI/EMJ/1...n04/em2408.sethi/em2408.sethi.html), 15/04/97.

Setchell, K.D.R. *Non steroidal estrogens of dietary origin: Possible roles in Hormone Dependent Disease.* American Journal of Clinical Nutrition, 40. 1989.

Setwright, R. *The natural alternative to Hormone Replacement Therapy.* Get Well (URL: http://www.getwell.com), 1996, 27.01.97.

Smith, Dr. M. and I. Smith. *Dr Mike Smith's Postbag, HRT.* Kyle Cathie Limited, London. 1993.

Smith, Dr. T.(ed). *The New Macmillan guide to Family Health.* Macmillan, London. 1989.

Smyth, A. *The menopause: make the change without HRT.* Here's Health, London. 09/93.

Stamphner, M.J. and G.A. Colditz. *Post Menopausal Estrogen Therapy and Cardiovascular Disease.* New England Journal of Medicine, 325(11). 1991.

Stevens, C. *Get into print: A guide to producing, publishing and selling your own books.* New Caxton Press, Bristol. 1992.

Stevens C.A. and A. Morris, G. Sargent. *Health information: a role for public access systems?* Journal of Information Science, 23(3). 1997.

Stevens C.A and A. Morris, G. Sargent. *Internet health information services.* The Electronic Library, 14(2). 1996.

Symposium Report. Hormonal Replacement Therapy (HRT). European Menopause Journal 3(2). 1996. (URL: http://www.medscape.com/PMSI/EMJ/1...dermooren/em3108.vandermooren.html), 20/02/97.

Symposium Report. *State of the Art Practical HRT.* European Menopause Journal 3(2). 1996. (URL: http://www.medscape.com/PMSI/EMJ/1...6.kenemans/em0302.06.kenemans.html), 20/02/97.

Symposium Report. *Today's issues in HRT.* European Menopause Journal 2(4). 1995. (URL: http://www.medscape.com/PMSI/EMJ/1...n04/em2410.marty/em2410.marty.html), 20/02/97.

Tang, MX and D. Jacobs, Y.Sherri, K Marder, P Schofield, B Gurkind, H Andrews, R Mayeux. *Effect of oestrogen during menopause on risk and age at onset of Alzheimer's disease.* The Lancet, 348. 1996.

Toscani, M.R. *Evaluating and creating effective patient education programmes.* Drug Benefit Trends, 7(9). 1995. (URL: http://www.medscape.com/SCP/DBT/19...n09/d161.toscani/d161.toscani.html), 15/05/97.

Vandenbroucke J.P. and F.M. Helmerhorst. *Risk of venous thrombosis with hormone replacement therapy*. The Lancet, 348. 1996.

Vines, G. *The challenge to HRT*. New Scientist. 23/10/93.

Watson, N.R. and J.W. Studd, T. Garnett, M Savvas, P. Milligan. *Bone loss after hysterectomy with ovarian conservation*. European Menopause Journal, 3(1). 1996. (URL: http://www.medscape.com/PMSI/EMJ/1...07.genazzani/em3107.genazzani.html), 02/02/97.

Warhusrt, Dr. M. Introduction to hormone disrupting chemicals. (URL: http://easyweb.easynet.co.uk/~mwarhusrt/oestrogenic.html) 16/10/96, 27/01/97.

Westcott, P. *HRT - is it all it's cracked up to be?* Here's Health. London. 11/91.

Williams, G. *Using the Internet to attract inward investment and tourism*. Electronic Public Information Provision, Fifth Annual Seminar. Loughborough University of Technology. 09/95.

Williams, G. *Electronic public information provision*; Fifth Annual Seminar; Loughborough University of Technology; September 1995.

Wilson, Dr R.C.D. *Understanding HRT and the Menopause*. Consumers Association Ltd, London. 1992.

Women's Health. *Alternative medicine - promoting good health.* Women's Health, London. 1993.

Women's Health. *Coping with heavy bleeding.* Women's Health, London. 1995.

Women's Health. *Fibroids.* Women's Health, London. 1995.

Women's Health. *HRT*. Women's Health, London. 1995.

Women's Health. *Hysterectomy*. Women's Health, London. 1995.

Women's Health. *The Menopause*. Women's Health, London, 1995.

Women's Health. *Ovaries - what can go wrong?* Women's Health, London. 1995.

Wren, B.G. *Hormonal replacement therapy and breast cancer*. European Menopause Journal, 2(4). 1995. (URL: http://www.medscape.com/PMSI/EMJ/1...2.n04/em2404.wren/em2404.wren.html), 20/02/97.

Young, L. and M Humphrey. *Cognitive Methods of preparing women for hysterectomy: Does a booklet help?* British Journal of Clinical Psychology, 24. 1985.

Young, P. *Health hazard women can no longer ignore*. Readers Digest. London. 06/95.

Appendices

Appendix 1 - List Of Support Organisations Contacted - (1997)

Amarant Trust, 11-13 Charterhouse Buildings, London, EC1M 7AN.
Menopause and HRT Charity, specialising in counselling who provide a list of Well Woman clinics and menopause clinics. The telephone helpline in London is staff by specialist nurses.

Health Information Service, Telephone - 088 665544.
A national service that has local centres. Offers information on a wide range of health related issues.

Margaret Pyke Centre, 15 Bateman Buildings, Soho Square, London, WIV 5TW, Telephone - 0171 734 9351.
Offers women an assessment as to their suitability for HRT.

Marie Stopes Centres, 108 Whitfield Street, London, W1P 6BE, Telephone - 0171 388 2585.
Offers the 'Menocheck' to assess hormone levels.

National Osteoporosis Society, PO Box 10, Radstock, Bath, BA3 3YB, Telephone - 01761 432472.
Provides up to date information on all aspects of osteoporosis, including information on the menpause, HRT, and exercise. Produces information packs on hysterectomy, HRT and calcium. The helpline is manned by specialist nurses.

The Endometriosis Society, 35 Belgrave Square, London, SW1X, 8QB, Telephone - 0171 235 4137.

Women's Health, 52 Featherstone Street, London, EC1Y 8RT, Telephone - 0171 251 6580.
Women's Health is committed to providing health information from a women's centred point of view, specifically to enable women to make an informed choice about health issues. There are leaflets available on hysterectomy and HRT.

The British Menopause Society, 36 West Street, Marlow, Bucks, SL7 2NB, Telephone 01628 890199.
Supports the advancement of knowledge, interest, and study of all matters connected with the menopause, to provide high standards of training for those involved in advising women.

Appendix 2 - WWW Site Structure

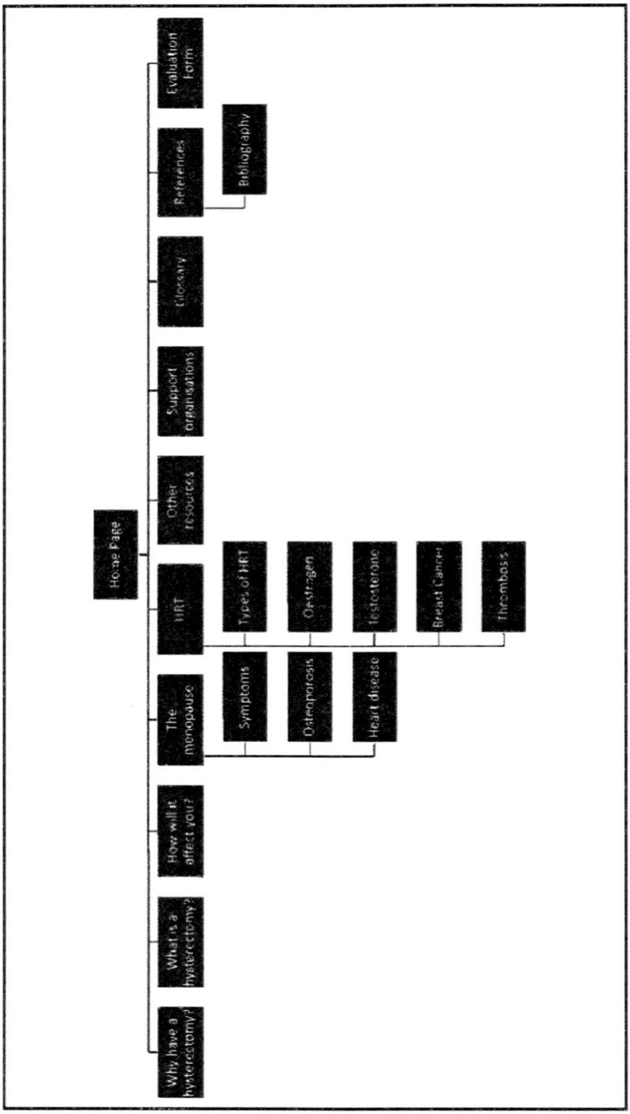

Appendix 3 - Books Currently (1997) In Print In The Uk

Books for Patients

Barber, S. Hysterectomy, woman to woman. R.R Bowker, USA, 1995.

Bigrigg, A and J. Smith. Hysterectomy. A guide to menstrual disorders. Headway, UK, 1994.

Butterworth, J. Hysterectomy. Thorsons, UK, 1995.

Coney, S. and L. Potter. Hysterectomy, Reed Publishing NZ, New Zealand, 1990.

Cox, K. Well-informed Patients Guide to Hysterectomy. Dell Publishing Company, USA, 1991.

Cutler, W.B. Hysterectomy, Before and After: A comprehensive guide to peventing, preparing for and maximising health after hysterectomy. Harper Collins Publishers, UK, 1990.

DeCosta, C. All about hysterectomy. Australia, 1994.

Delthia, T.R. Hysterectomy and You. Budlong Press Company, UK, 1994.

Dennerstein, L. and C. Wood, A. Westmore. Hysterectomy, new options and advances. OUP Australia and New Zealand, Australia, 1995.

Dickson, A. and Henriques, N. Hysterectomy: the woman's view. Quartet Books, UK, 1994.

Elliott, P. Hysterectomy. Family Doctor Publications, UK, 1995.

Goldfarb, H. and J. Grief. The no-hysterectomy option: your body - your choice. John Wiley and Sons, USA, 1997.

Greenberg M.D. Making a Choice. Berkley Publishing Group, USA, 1993.

Gressor, M. So You're having a Hysterectomy. Gore and Osment Publications, UK, 1993.

Haas, A. and H. McLean. Recovering from a hysterectomy. HarperCollins Publishers Inc, USA, 1995.

Haslett, S. and M. Jennings. Hysterectomy and Vaginal Repair. 3rd. Ed. Beaconsfield Publishers, UK, 1992.

Hayman, S. Hysterectomy: What it is and how to cope successfully with it. Sheldon Press, UK, 1994.

Hoffman, M.S. Hysterectomy: a guide for women. Women's Health Service, USA, 1996.

Hufnagel, V.G. and S.K. Golant. No more hysterectomies. Plume Books, UK, 1989.

Lindeque, C. Hysterectomy: a new life. Academia Publishers, UK, 1992.

Royal Marsden NHS Trust. Hysterectomy: Your questions answered. Royal Marsden NHS Trust, 1986.

Simpkin, S. The case against hysterectomy. Pandora, UK, 1996.

Smith, J. and A. Bigrigg. Hysterectomy and alternative operations. Arnold, UK 1994.

Strausz, I.K. You don't need a hysterectomy: new and effective ways of avoiding major surgery. Addison Wesley Longman, US, 1994.

Swanney, A. Health, happiness and hormones: One woman's journey towards health after hysterectomy. Starburst Publishers Inc, USA, 1996.

West, S. and P. Dranov. The hysterectomy hoax. Doubleday and Company, UK, 1994.

Wigfall-Williams, W. Hysterectomy: learning the facts, coping with the feelings, facing the future. Michael Kesend Publishing, USA, 1986.

UK Magazines Contacted

Here's Health. BPC Magazines Ltd, London

Zest. The National Magazine Company, London

Woman's Weekly. BPC Magazines Ltd, London

Woman's Own. IPC Magazines Ltd, London

Bella. H Bauer Publishing, London

Options. IPC Magazines Ltd, London

Woman, BPC Magazines Ltd, London

SHE. The National Magazine Company, London

Woman and Home. IPC Magazines Ltd, London.

Appendix 4 - Internet Sites About Hysterectomy Defined By Type

Support and Information

Hysterectomy Support Pages, 18th August 1997,
URL: http://www.ukonline.co.ik/linda.newall/index.htm

Sans-Uteri, 18th August 1997. URL: http://www.2cowherd.net/findings

Shaes Pages, General articles about hysterectomy, 18th August 1997
URL: http://users.vnet.net/shae/wissues/hysterectomy.html

Sales

Myomectomy, safe and effective alternative to hysterectomy, 18th August 1997.
URL: http://www.netreach.net/~hysterectomyedu

FexRx, device manufacturer, 18th August 1997. URL: http://www.fexrx.com

Mailing/Discussion Lists

Creativity Cafe, 18th August 1997, URL: http://www.creativity.net/CCafe/

Professional sites

Hysterectomy: a primer, 18th August 1997.
URL:
ttp://www.havorford.edu/biology/wmbweb/topics/hysterectomy.html
.

Appendix 5 - Tables

Table 1

Is the type of hysterectomy performed affected by the reason for it?

Type of hysterectomy by reason

	Total	Partial	Lining	Other
Heavy Bleeding	44%	44%	12%	
Fibroids	64%	36%		
Uterine Cancer	100%			
Ovarian Cancer	100%			
Cervical Cancer	50%	50%		
Endometriosis	77%	15%		8%
Prolapse	20%	60%	20%	
Other	60%	40%		

Tables 2

Is the information used affected by the source of the respondents?

Source by information received about hysterectomy (Q.7)

Subject	Personal	Women's Health	Stamford	Wokingham	Here's Health
About Operation	17%	26%	23%	11%	23%
Before Operation	12%	18%	47%	12%	11%
Operation	9%	29%	32%	9%	21%
Recovery	12%	37.5%	26.5%	8%	16%
HRT	12%	28%	36%	8%	16%
None	12.5%	50%	12.5%		25%

Source by ease of understanding (Q.8)

Understand easily	Personal	Women's Health	Stamford	Wokingham	Here's Health
Yes	10%	32%	32%	7%	19%
A little difficult	27%	45.5%	9%	9%	9.5%
Very difficult		100%			

Source by discussion with GP (Q.9)

Visits with GP	Personal	Women's Health	Stamford	Wokingham	Here's Health
1-3 times	15%	37%	22%	6%	20%
3-6 times		33%	67%		
6+ times		33%	33%	34%	
No need	14%	43%	28%		15%

Source by questions answered fully (Q.10)

Questions answered fully	Personal	Women's Health	Stamford	Wokingham	Here's Health
Yes	6%	31%	34%	13%	16%
Some of the time	18%	35%	23%		24%
Not very well	22%	67%			11%

Source by preparation for surgery (Q.11)

Questions answered fully	Personal	Women's Health	Stamford	Wokingham	Here's Health
Yes	9%	8%	48%	9%	26%
Partly	24%	39%	14%	9%	14%
No	6%	75%	6%		13%

Source by HRT subject information received (Q.12)

Subject	Personal	Women's Health	Stamford	Wokingham	Here's Health
Breast Cancer		33%	33%	9%	25%
Osteoporosis	5%	35%	30%	10%	20%
Heart Disease		22%	56%		22%
Types of HRT		46%	9%	18%	27%
Alternatives to HRT	13%	39%	24%	6%	18%
Menopause	25%	12.5%	50%		12.5%
None from GP	16%	47%	21%	3%	13%
None from Consultant	17%	41.5%	23.5%	3%	15%

Source by who gave the most information (Q.13)

Main Source	Personal	Women's Health	Stamford	Wokingham	Here's Health
GP		27%	37%	18%	18%
Practice Nurse		100%			
Well Woman Clinic		100%			
Menopause Clinic		100%			
Consultant	8%	17%	33%	9%	33%
Hospital Nurse	17%	50%	16%		17%
No-one	22%	37%	22%	4%	15%

Source by when was most information received (Q.14)

When was it given	Personal	Women's Health	Stamford	Wokingham	Here's Health
Before the operation		33%	17%	17%	33%
In hospital	12.5%	62.5%	25%		
After the operation	4%	42%	25%	8%	21%
None was given	23%	32%	23%	4%	18%

Source by type of information given (Q.15)

Information type	Personal	Women's Health	Stamford	Wokingham	Here's Health
Company leaflets	12.5%	50%	25%	12.5%	
Hospita/GP leaflets	13%	27%	40%	7%	13%
Support Organisatio ns		37.5%	25%	12.5%	25%
Videos		33%	67%		
None given	21%	37%	17%	4%	21%

Source by alternative sources of information (Q.20)

Alternative Source	Personal	Women's Health	Stamford	Wokingham	Here's Health
Friends	9%	39%	22%	13%	17%
Library	6%	65%	6%	6%	17%
Support Organisatio n	8%	73%	4%		15%
H.I.S	17%	50%			33%
Women's Centre	75%				25%
Media	10%	37%	19%	6%	28%
Telephone Lines		62.5%			37.5%
Internet	33%		33%		34%
Family		40%		40%	20%
Other	20%	60%			20%
None used	40%		60%		

Source by support organisations known of (Q.21)

Organisatio ns	Personal	Women's Health	Stamford	Wokingham	Here's Health
Menopause Society	12.5%	62.5%	12.5%		12.5%
Hysterectom y Network	9%	82%	4.5%	4.5%	
Osteoporosi s Society	20%	52%	8%	8%	12%

Source by preferred place of information (Q.23)

Place	Personal	Women's Health	Stamford	Wokingham	Here's Health
GP Surgery	17%	31%	33%	5%	14%
Hospital		100%			
Self help group					
Library		67%			100%
Internet	100%				33%

Tables 3

Is the type of Hormone Replacement Therapy used affected by the type of information received about HRT?

Type of HRT by information received on HRT (Q.12)

Subject	Tablets	Patches	Cream	Implant	Other
Breast Cancer	80%	20%			
Osteoporosis	78%	17%		5%	
Heart Disease	87.5%	12.5%			
Types of HRT	70%	10%	10%		10%
Alternatives to HRT					
Menopause	100%				
None - GP	60%	30%		5%	5%
None - Consultant	63%	26%		5%	6%

Type of HRT by alternative sources of information (Q.20)

Alternative Source	Tablets	Patches	Cream	Implant	Other
Friends	57%	29%	7%	7%	
Library	36%	43%	7%	7%	7%
Support Organisatio n	47%	35%		6%	12%
H.I.S	33%	33%			34%
Women's Centre	25%	50%			25%
Media	70%	22%			8%
Telephone Lines	60%	20%			
Internet	67%				
Family	40%	40%	20%		
Other	43%	29%	14%	14%	
None used	57%	43%			

Tables 4

Does the type of information received affect whether women will take Hormone Replacement Therapy?

Taking HRT by source (Q.1)

Source	Taking HRT	Not taking HRT
Personal	50%	50%
Women's Health	62.5%	37.5%
Stamford	67%	33%
Wokingham	50%	50%
Here's Health	64%	26%

Taking HRT by age group

Source	Taking HRT	Not taking HRT
20-30		100%
30-40	67%	33%
40-50	65%	35%
50+	56%	44%

Taking HRT by who gave the most information (Q. 13)

Who gave information	Taking HRT	Not taking HRT
GP	82%	18%
Practice nurse	100%	
Well woman clinic	50%	50%
Menopause clinic	100%	
Consultant	67%	33%
Hospital nurse	100%	
No-one	41%	59%

Taking HRT by HRT subject (Q.12)

Subject	Taking HRT	Not taking HRT
Breast Cancer	75%	25%
Osteoporosis	85%	15%
Heart Disease	89%	11%
Types of HRT	91%	9%
Alternatives to HRT		
Menopause	62.5%	37.5%
None - GP	50%	50%
None - Consultant	50%	50%

Taking of HRT by alternative sources of information (Q.20)

Alternative Source	Taking HRT	Not taking HRT
Friends	48%	52%
Library	71%	29%
Support Organisation	58%	42%
H.I.S	67%	33%
Women's Centre	25%	75%
Media	66%	34%
Telephone Lines	50%	50%
Internet	67%	33%
Family	80%	20%
Other	70%	30%
None used	70%	30%

* 9 7 8 1 7 3 9 4 2 7 2 0 7 *
ND - #0381 - 140926 - C0 - 210/148/11 - PB - 9781739427207 - Gloss Lamination